ELIZABETHAN
ACTING

ELIZABETHAN ACTING

BY

B. L. JOSEPH

Second Edition

OXFORD UNIVERSITY PRESS

1964

Oxford University Press, Amen House, London E.C.4

GLASGOW NEW YORK TORONTO MELBOURNE WELLINGTON
BOMBAY CALCUTTA MADRAS KARACHI LAHORE DACCA
CAPE TOWN SALISBURY NAIROBI IBADAN ACCRA
KUALA LUMPUR HONG KONG

First published 1951 in the
OXFORD ENGLISH MONOGRAPHS

PRINTED IN GREAT BRITAIN

Preface to Second Edition

THE first edition of this work contained an account of the part played by rhetorical delivery in the scheme of humanist learning. This is not strictly relevant to an understanding of the art of Elizabethan acting. It has therefore been deleted from this edition. The first edition's tentative discussion of standards which might be applied in evaluating Elizabethan plays has been omitted for the same reason, and because it is a subject requiring full treatment in its own right.

The new edition takes into account evidence and arguments brought forward in the last twelve years. It also records developments in my understanding of the subject as the result of teaching and discussion academically, supplemented by what I have learned from practical work with actors and acting students.

The same picture of Elizabethan acting is given here as in the first edition. There are alterations of emphasis, but the method is fundamentally unchanged. I still use renaissance writings on the art of action off the stage to supplement the scanty surviving accounts of acting on it. To do this, however, is by no means to suggest that Elizabethan acting was formal or stereotyped, still less that the actor was any kind of automaton. The terms 'lively', 'natural', and 'familiar' are used by Elizabethans of the orator as well as the player. Both are described as feeling emotion truthfully and intensely; each was trained to allow emotion to communicate itself completely and naturally in voice, countenance, and movement. Rhetorical delivery at school meant that boys were required to act naturally, as if they really were the persons whom they represented, when reciting an episode from a narrative poem or even a Latin dialogue or a scene from a play. The rhetorician who followed Quintilian tapped the resources of his emotional life by methods still used in the modern theatre and advocated by Stanislavski and his followers.

Comparatively little emphasis was given to these aspects of rhetorical delivery and stage-playing in the first edition. This was not in order to suggest that acting was formal. I was interested simply in establishing the validity of sources hitherto neglected. The first part of the book was therefore concerned with evidence that what was done by the orator was also done by the actor, though the reverse was not true. Without emphasizing that the actor was identified, but quoting much evidence which shows that he was, and never at any time declaring his art to have been formal, I then concentrated on applying the new body of sources to the fundamental problem of how the Elizabethan was able to appear to be the character he represented while doing justice to the qualities of his lines judged purely as literature. Now, in this edition, I am taking the opportunity of emphasizing more forcibly the fact that the actor was identified, but that this helped rather than obstructed him in making the dramatist's art with words more manifest to the audience. A number of examples of Elizabethan dramatic speech have been analysed in the light of what is to be learned from rhetorical delivery, to explain how the Elizabethan actor created character out of his understanding of the words as literature and the speech of the imaginary person simultaneously. We learn to perceive that the relationship of word to word in his lines was for him a relationship of thinking, feeling and wanting to obtain an objective, all of which were communicated in his acting as a relationship of articulate sound, to which the audience responded as the literary product of the writer and as an expression of the inner life of the character.

Such virtues as this edition may be found to possess owe much to those persons with whom I have discussed the subject over many years, some few in the universities, but most in the theatres and theatre schools of this country. I shall restrict myself, however, to naming the following friends: Ian Bishop, Margaret Bury, Margaret Collins, Harry H. Corbett, James E. Cross, John Hale, Daphne Heard, Brian Holbeche, Bernard and Josephine Miles, Michael MacOwan, Duncan Ross, Elizabeth Shepherd, and Roy Thomas. The defects derive solely from me.

B. L. J.

University of Bristol
September 1962

Preface to First Edition

THE spelling of my sources has been maintained in quotation; but contractions have been expanded except for the ampersand. For major quotations from Shakespeare the text of the First Folio (1623) has been used: where it has been necessary to quote from one or other of the Quartos, the fact is noted.

It is simple to acknowledge the help received in writing this book; difficult to convey accurately the quality of my debt both to individuals and institutions. My first encouragement came from Professor E. C. Llewellyn of the University College of South Wales and Monmouthshire, to the Librarian of which, Mr. S. O. Moffet, and his Staff I owe more than they perhaps realize. During the early stages of this work I was guided and encouraged by Mr. Nevill Coghill. Later I have benefited from the comment and encouragement of Professor C. M. Bowra, Mr. J. B. Bamborough, Dr. Percy Simpson, Professor Lord David Cecil, and Professor J. R. R. Tolkien.

I have been fortunate enough to be able to understand from personal experience why so many prefaces bear witness to the help and kindness of the Staff of the Bodleian Library, of Mr. Strickland Gibson, Dr. Hunt, and Dr. Hassall.

I must emphasize the nature of my debt to Professor F. P. Wilson. I have benefited from his suggestions, and from his calling my attention to facts which I am confident I should otherwise have continued to overlook.

It is to the generosity of the University of Wales that I owe the leisure necessary for that large part of the work done during my tenure of a Fellowship.

B. L. J.

University of Bristol
April 1950

Contents

Plate

Note

The illustrations of rhetorical gestures of the hand have been taken from John Bulwer's *Chirologia* and *Chironomia* (1644).

CHAPTER ONE

External Action

THE few pre-Restoration accounts which have come down to us
make it clear that Elizabethan acting was not formal. The actor
was identified; he behaved as if he were the imaginary character
come to life; when he was successful this is how he was accepted
by his audience. The players 'appear to you to be the self-same
men' they represented, says one of the commendatory poems
prefixed to Heywood's *Apology for Actors* (1612).[1] In the work
itself, Heywood describes the effect of an actor playing a hero
from English history. It was as if the historical personage
were actually there, so far as the audience was concerned. 'What
English blood, seeing the person of any bold Englishman presented, and doth not hug his fame?' The audience responded to
the actor 'as being wrapt in contemplation'; it was 'as if the
personator were the man personated, so bewitching a thing is
lively and well-spirited action, that it hath power to new-mould
the hearts of the spectators'.[2]

'Did I not do it to the life?' asks Nero, in the anonymous play
of that name (1623), to be told that his acting was utterly
convincing:

> The very doing never was so lively
> As was this counterfeiting.[3]

Other references to acting use such terms as 'doing it to the
life', 'lively', and 'naturally'. There can be no doubt that actors
were judged according to their ability to appear 'the self-same
men'. The Prologue to *Ram Alley* (1609) sees the actor's art as

---

[1] By Arthur Hopton; sig. a1ᵛ.   [2] Sig. B4ʳ.
[3] Ed. Horne (III. ii), pp. 41 f. See D. Klein, 'Elizabethan Acting', *PMLA*, lxxi.
282.

to show

Things never done, with that true life,
That thoughts and wits should stand at strife,
Whether the things now shown be true,
Or whether we ourselves now do
The things we but present.[1]

Margaret in *A New Way To Pay Old Debts* (1625) tells Allworthy:

And, though but a young actor, second me
In doing to the life what he has plotted.   (IV. iii. 50–51.)[2]

Coriolanus objects unavailingly in Shakespeare's play:

You have put me now to such a part which never
I shall discharge to th' life.   (III. ii. 105–6.)

And Thomas Riley, who acted in *The Jealous Lovers*, is praised by the author, Thomas Randolph:

When thou dost act, men think it not a play,
But all they see is real.[3]

Sometimes the terminology might suggest to us today that the Elizabethans regarded the actor's art as one of pretending to feel, of appearing to, but not of really feeling. For instance, Hylus in Chapman's *The Widow's Tears* (1612) counterfeited 'preciously for accent and action, as if he felt the part he played'.[4] In *The Heir* (1620) Thomas May has Polymetes talk as if an acted passion were a false one. Roscio asks if he has seen 'A player passionate Hieronimo?' To which the reply is:

By th' mass, 'tis true. I have seen the knave paint grief
In such a lively colour, that for false
And acted passion he hath drawn true tears
From the spectators. Ladies in the boxes
Kept time with sighs and tears to his sad accents,
As he had truly been the man he seem'd.[5]

---

[1] *Hazlitt's Dodsley*, x. 269.
[2] Ed. Brooke and Paradise, *English Drama 1580–1642* (1933), p. 903.
[3] 'To his friend, Thomas Riley' (1632), *Poetical and Dramatic Works of Thomas Randolph*, ed. W. C. Hazlitt (1875), i. 60.
[4] (III. ii. 19–20.) Ed. Parrott (1914), p. 402.
[5] (I. i.) *Hazlitt's Dodsley*, xi. 514.

But the suggestions here that the actor's passion was false are completely contradicted by Hamlet's comments on the Player's 'action'. This actor really felt as if Hecuba mattered to him. What was feigned was not the passion, but the imagined concern with Troy and her queen. The feeling itself was real, and from it came all the details of the player's external appearance. To embody a fiction this man has been able to

> force his soul so to his own conceit
> That from her working all his visage wann'd;
> Tears in his eyes, distraction in's aspect,
> A broken voice, and his whole function suiting
> With forms to his conceit.
>
> (II. ii. 546–50.)

In truth it is 'all for nothing'. He is nothing to Hecuba, and Hecuba is nothing to him; but he weeps for her because he can imagine that she matters. What Stanislavski calls the magic 'if' has allowed the actor really to feel moved by her imagined agony. His 'whole function'—voice, face, attitude, gesture—expresses what he feels. This is what happens when an actor is identified.

It was for this kind of acting that Burbage and Alleyn were praised in their own times. Each seemed to become an entirely different person according to the demands of every separate role. Heywood says that Alleyn could 'vary' so well that he was 'Proteus for shapes'.[1] And Burbage's power of identifying himself with each individual role has impressed the writer of his elegy:

> He's gone, and with him what a world are dead,
> Which he reviv'd to be revived so.
> No more young Hamlet, old Hieronymo.
> King Lear, the grieved Moor, and more beside,
> That liv'd in him, have now for ever died.
> Oft have I seen him leap into the grave,
> Suiting the person which he seem'd to have
> Of a sad lover with so true an eye,
> That there I would have sworn he meant to die.

---

[1] See Marlowe, *The Jew of Malta and The Massacre at Paris*, ed. Bennett (1931), p. 28.

Oft have I seen him play this part in jest,
So lively that spectators and the rest
Of his sad crew, whilst he but seem'd to bleed,
Amaz'd, thought even then he died indeed.[1]

Richard Flecknoe, writing just after the Restoration, does not
have quite the authority of a contemporary. But he, too, speaks
of the strength of identification with which Burbage played a role.
For him Burbage was 'a delightful Proteus, so wholly transform-
ing himself into his part, and putting off himself with his clothes,
as he never (not so much as in the tiring-house) assumed himself
again until the play was done'. Stanislavski would have approved
wholeheartedly of this, and of Burbage listening and responding
to others when silent on the stage himself, always as if he were
the character come to life. He was 'an excellent actor still, never
falling in his part when he had done speaking, but with his looks
and gesture maintaining it still unto the heighth, he imagining
Age quod agis only spoke to him'.[2]

Randolph's praise of Riley, part of which has been quoted,
concentrates on his 'Protean' quality:

> I have seen a Proteus, that can take
> What shape he please, and in an instant make
> Himself to anything: be that or this
> By voluntary metamorphosis.   .
> . . . O, that day
> (When I had cause to blush that this poor thing
> Did kiss a Queen's hand, and salute a King)
> How often had I lost thee! I could find
> One of thy stature, but in every kind
> Alter'd from him I knew; nay, I in thee
> Could all professions and all passions see.
> When thou art pleas'd to act an angry part,
> Thou fright'st the audience; and with nimble art
> Turn'd lover, thou dost that so lively too,
> Men think that Cupid taught thee how to woo.[3]

[1] Repr. Sir Edmund Chambers, *The Elizabethan Stage* (1923), ii. 309.
[2] *A Short Discourse of the English Stage* (1664), sig. G7^r.
[3] Op. cit. i. 60.

'What we see him personate, we think truly done before us', is said in praise of *An Excellent Actor* in the *Character* attributed to John Webster, the playwright. Moreover, according to this account, the excellent Elizabethan actor not only appeared as if he were the very man whom he represented, but showed in his acting everything that was to be commended in the delivery of an orator. There was this important difference, however; whatever was good when it was done by an orator was much better in the player's acting. 'Whatsoever is commendable in the grave orator is most exquisitely perfect in him; for by a full and significant action of body he charms our attention.'[1]

Some fifty years later, Flecknoe also speaks of Burbage as one whose acting involved what was done by contemporary orators. Not only is the actor praised for being so utterly identified, but he 'had all the parts of an excellent orator, (animating his words with speaking, and speech with action)'.[2] And here Flecknoe is supported by that Elizabethan playgoer, Sir Richard Baker, who actually saw Burbage and Alleyn perform. His praise of their acting is followed by the remark: 'We may well acknowledge that gracefulness of action is the greatest pleasure of a play; seeing it is the greatest pleasure of (the art of pleasure) Rhetoric.'[3]

Elizabethan acting involved in the actor the ability to 'force his soul . . . to his own conceit' coupled at the same time with 'whatsoever is commendable in the grave orator'. Thomas Wright assures us of this in a plain explicit statement quite void of ambiguity. He says that for the most part the delivery of the renaissance orator was the same as that of the actor. 'In the substance of external action for most part orators and stage-players agree.'[4] Like the writer of *An Excellent Actor*, Wright is convinced that the actors were much the better.

By 'orator' the Elizabethans did not necessarily mean only a person who made speeches or delivered orations. The word was used of anyone skilled in the art of using language, whether he

---

[1] *New and Choice Characters of Several Authors* (1615), 6th ed., p. 147.
[2] Op. cit., sig. G7ʳ.   [3] *Theatrum Triumphans* (1670,) pp. 34 f.
[4] *The Passions of the Mind in General* (1604), p. 179.

wrote or spoke fiction or non-fiction, in prose or verse. By 'external action' was meant the trained use of voice, countenance, and gesture to communicate what had already been expressed in words by the author, or was now being expressed by the speaker. 'External action' was involved in the reading of non-dramatic verse aloud as in the declamation of a speech. It was one of the accomplishments of the polished, educated man; it was taught in school and university and was practised by lawyers and statesmen, by public orators at official entries, by the participators in triumphs, pageants, and public shows. Jasper Mayne celebrated John Donne's 'action':

> Yet have I seen thee in the pulpit stand,
> Where one might take notes from thy look and hand,
> And from thy speaking action bear away
> More sermon than some teachers use to say.
> Such was thy carriage, and thy gesture such,
> As could divide the heart, and conscience touch:
> Thy motion did confute, and one might see
> An error vanquish'd by delivery.[1]

There was nothing stereotyped, stiff or formal about this 'external action'. It was not an esoteric art of conventional gesture. On the contrary, 'natural', 'familiar', and 'lively' are the words used of it just as they are the words used of stage-playing. Thomas Heywood chooses 'natural' and 'familiar' to describe what is for him the orator's 'gracious and bewitching action'. It is 'a natural and familiar motion of the head, the hand, the body and a moderate and fit countenance suitable to all the rest'.[2] John Bulwer gives a detailed account of the 'natural and familiar motion of . . . the hand' in his *Chirologia* and *Chironomia* published together in 1644. He insists that delivery must not be stereotyped. What might suit one man, he says, is not to be copied slavishly by another; each must develop his own individual action.

In all action nature bears the greatest sway: every man must consider his own nature and temperament . . . One action becomes

[1] See J. Bulwer, *Chironomia* (1644), p. 20.   [2] Sig. C4ʳ.

one man, and another kind of behaviour another. That which one does without art cannot wholly be delivered by art; for there is a kind of hidden and ineffable reason, which to know is the head of art.

Some people lack essential grace despite a thorough knowledge of all the details of the art of delivery; in others even the 'vices of rhetoric' are delightful. 'A rhetorician must know himself, yet not by common precepts; but he must take counsel of nature for the framing of the complexional and individual properties of his hand.'

Bulwer emphasizes one point which establishes beyond doubt the certainty that for him 'action' was anything but a formal, stereotyped system of gesture. Every orator should develop his own external action in accordance with the needs of his own personality: 'No man can put off his own and put on another's nature.'[1]

Both orator and stage-player were expected to be natural and unaffected in action. One writer, who calls for 'apt composition' of the fingers, warns that 'conceit in it is uncomely'.[2] Bulwer denounces affectation: 'Shun affectation, for all affectation is odious.'[3] So, too, we can read disapproval of the 'overdoing' stage-player who 'affects grossly': such acting is 'so far forc'd from life' that it betrays itself 'to be altogether artificial'.[4] An 'unfeign'd passion' is best deciphered by 'unartificial truth', says Alphonso in *The Gentleman Usher* (1606).[5] From Lodovico in *May Day* (1611) we hear that the way to act a 'dissembling part' is 'in the most modest judgment and passing naturally'.[6]

The grammar school teachers set out to train their pupils to act 'passing naturally'. Not only when they were performing plays, but when they were reading and pronouncing Latin dialogues, the boys were instructed to act 'lively and naturally'.

---

[1] *Chiron.*, p. 143.
[2] *A Brief Sum of the Arts of Logic, Sophistry and Rhetoric* (MS. Ashmole 768), p. 541.　　　　　　　　　　　　　　　　[3] *Chiron.*, p. 138.
[4] Chapman, *The Widow's Tears* (1612), ed. Parrott (IV. i. 106–7), p. 407.
[5] Ibid. (I. i. 232–3), p. 241.
[6] Ibid. (III. iii. 73–75), p. 203.

One writer on teaching declares that 'what they cannot utter well in Latin, cause them first to do it lively in English'. The master should then let them see where they had gone wrong by imitating their mistakes. 'Then pronounce it rightly and naturally before them likewise, that they may perceive the difference to be ashamed of the one, and take a delight in the other.'[1]

This may not be the best way of teaching this art, but it shows that orators were expected to be natural and lively in delivery. Action has the greatest effect upon an audience, Bulwer reminds us, 'when they perceive all things to flow, as it were, out of the liquid current of Nature'.[2]

For the orator as for the stage-player the function of 'external action' was to express naturally and completely what was felt truthfully by the speaker. Theory insisted and practice confirmed that what is experienced within determines what is shown without. Bulwer compiled his treatises because he and his times looked upon the hand in delivery as 'receiving good intelligence of the pathetical motions of the mind'. As a result of responding to the emotions—'the pathetical motions of the mind'—the hand becomes 'a summary or index, wherein the speaking habits thereof significantly appear, representing in their appearance the present posture of the fancy'.[3]

External action reveals the inner cause which both prompts and determines it. Gestures combined with speaking are doubly effective; for the 'actions' alone, 'and by themselves do speak and show the mental springs from whence they do naturally arise'.[4] As distinct from 'significant action', the lineaments of the body 'disclose the disposition and inclination of the mind in general'. But the gestures are more precise; in addition to revealing the general disposition, they 'do further disclose the present humour and state of the mind and will'.[5] Stage-players reveal in their acting the state of the character's 'will'. The action of the orator in the Renaissance served the same purpose for the speaker.

---

[1] John Brinsley, *Ludus Literarius: Or The Grammar School* (1612), p. 214.
[2] *Chiron.*, p. 138.   [3] *Chirol.*, p. 157.
[4] *Chiron.*, pp. 16 f.   [5] *Chirol.*, sig. A5ʳ.

Action as a whole was to function as 'an external image of an internal mind'. It was a 'shadow of affections' (a reflection of emotions), which are communicated in voice, countenance, and gesture of the body; these are 'three springs which flow from one fountain, called *vox*, *vultus*, *vita*, voice, countenance, life'.[1]

The orator off the stage and the actor on it had to be able to express in action what was really felt. 'The passion which is in our breast', says Wright, 'is the fountain and origin of all external actions.'[2] Action was not an external applied from without; on and off the stage, for player and for orator it was what happened to voice, face and body when emotion was felt and communicated so adequately as to stir up its counterpart in the audience. 'Action, then, universally is a natural or artificial moderation, qualification, or composition of the voice, countenance and gesture, proceeding from some passion, and apt to stir up the like.'[3]

Like the player's function, that of the orator 'suited with forms to' what was being experienced within. Where Hamlet says this of the player, Wright asserts of the orator:

As the internal affection [i.e. emotion] is more vehement, so the external persuasion will be more potent: for the passion in the persuader seemeth to me to resemble the wind a trumpeter bloweth in at one end of the trumpet, and in what manner it proceedeth from him, so it issueth forth at the other end, and cometh to our ears; even so the passion proceedeth from the heart, and is blown about the body, face, eyes, hands, voice, and so by gestures passeth into our eyes, and by sounds into our ears.[4]

In laying such stress on emotion as the natural source of delivery, Englishmen of the Renaissance subscribed to a tradition which stretched back at least as far as ancient Rome. 'Cicero expressly teacheth it is almost impossible for an orator to stir up a passion in his auditors except he be first affected with the same passion himself.'[5] Elizabethan speakers were taught that it was impossible for the listener to 'sorrow, hate, envy or fear anything, that he should be induced to compassion or weeping, except all

---

[1] Wright, p. 176.
[2] Ibid., p. 174.
[3] Ibid., p. 176.
[4] Ibid., p. 174.
[5] Ibid., p. 179.

those motions which the orator would stir up in the judge, be first imprinted and marked in the orator himself'.[1]

It is not generally realized that Quintilian actually advises his readers to evoke emotion truthfully within themselves by one of the methods taught by Stanislavski: that is by means of what are called 'private images' by some modern actors and teachers of acting:

But how are we to generate these emotions in ourselves, since emotion is not in our power? I will try to explain as best I may. There are certain experiences which the Greeks call φαντασίαι, and the Romans *visiones*, whereby things absent are presented to our imagination with such extreme vividness that they seem actually to be before our very eyes. It is the man who is really sensitive to such impressions who will have the greatest power over the emotions.

Quintilian agrees with modern theorists and practitioners of acting that this 'is a power which all may readily acquire if they will'. He continues: 'We must identify ourselves with the persons of whom we complain that they have suffered grievous, un- merited and bitter misfortune.'

The importance of this statement cannot be exaggerated; what Quintilian had to say about the art of oratory in general, and of 'action' in particular, affected the Elizabethans powerfully, both in theory and practice. They are for ever referring to him, and his *Institutio Oratoria* was known in every school. This section of the work alone should be sufficient to disabuse us of any notion that Elizabethan 'action' was 'formal', as oratory or as stage-playing. The Elizabethans were guided by Quintilian in their emphasis on the need for boys to speak dialogues and read plays and poems in class as if they were themselves the persons speaking. 'Even in the schools it is desirable that the student should be moved by his theme and should imagine it to be true.'

Quintilian himself ascribed much of his own success to his ability to feel truthfully and powerfully:

I have thought it necessary not to conceal these considerations

[1] Wright, p. 172.

from my reader, since they have contributed to the acquisition of such reputation for talent as I possess or once possessed. I have frequently been so moved while speaking, that I have not merely been wrought upon to tears, but have turned pale and shown all the symptoms of genuine grief.[1]

It was for a civilization permeated by this attitude to 'action' that Bulwer was writing. He took Quintilian for granted when asserting that it was 'a thing nature hath so appointed' that all men are 'stirred and moved by the same motives of the mind, and do in others understand and take notice of the same moving demonstrations, by experience judging and approving in themselves those affections that outwardly appear to work upon others'.[2]

This was one of the reasons why plays were acted in school and university. A speaker's delivery depended upon what he was genuinely feeling; and even academic performances in those days could develop the ability to feel emotion and express it in action. At school, as Quintilian directed, boys were instructed not only to identify themselves with characters in plays, but even with the individual speakers in the dialogues pronounced in the learning of Latin. In *Ludus Literarius*, Brinsley says that the master should teach his pupils 'to pronounce every matter according to the nature of it, so much as you can; chiefly where persons or other things are feigned to speak'. In any kind of writing this should be the custom 'where persons or other things' have been imagined as speaking. Taking the boys through the collection, *Confabulatiunculae pueriles*, the teacher ought to 'cause them to utter every dialogue lively, as if they themselves were the persons which did speak in that dialogue, and so in every other speech, to imagine themselves to have occasion to utter the very same thing'.[3]

'Lively', the word used here of uttering every dialogue, is the word used of stage-playing. And the actor, like the schoolboy, had to imagine himself 'to have occasion to utter the very same

---

[1] Book VI, section 27, tr. Butler (1921), ii. 433 ff.
[2] *Chiron.*, p. 4.   [3] pp. 213 ff.

thing' as had been given to the character whom he was playing. Like Stanislavski and anybody else who understands the nature of acting, Brinsley talks of speakers behaving 'as if' they were the actual persons of the dialogue with 'occasion' to use the words allotted to them. If nothing else shows that these orators in training practised what is essentially acting, the matter is put beyond doubt by this last direction. The boys did what the stage-player does now, and what he did in Shakespeare's day.

Throughout the ages, actors have perfected their art by accurately observing how people really behave in life. David Garrick, who was renowned for the accuracy of his observation, as for the truth and intensity of his acting, used to say that his playing of Lear's madness owed much to his having carefully noted the behaviour of an old man who lost his reason as the result of having inadvertently dropped a baby grandchild to death from an upper-story window.[1] The Elizabethan 'orator' was also counselled to observe people in real life, and to base his 'action' upon their behaviour. Wright says to 'look upon other men appassionate', noticing 'how they demean themselves in passions, and observe what and how they speak in mirth, sadness, ire, fear, hope &c., what motions are stirring in the eyes, hands, body, &c.' His whole point is that the actual emotion felt within decides the appearance of 'eyes, hands, body, &c.'.

The 'action' of rage is best observed in 'witty women when they chide', because 'they let nature work in her kind'—let nature express itself naturally. 'Their voice is loud and sharp, and consequently apt to cut, which is proper to ire and hatred, which wish ill and intend revenge: their gestures are frequent, their faces inflamed, their eyes glowing, their reasons hurry one in the neck of another, they with their fingers number the wrongs offered them, the harms, injuries, disgraces and what not, thought, said and done against them.' An orator could perfect his delivery by watching and learning from such things. Such 'action' would have to be toned down, 'their excess be vicious';

---

[1] See M. Barton, *David Garrick* (1948), pp. 56 f.; T. Davies, *Memoirs of the Life of David Garrick Esq.* (1780), ii. 81 f.

but despite that 'excess', the 'furious fashion' of these women 'will serve for a good mean to perceive the external manage of this passion' for one overriding reason; in them 'nature' works 'in her kind'; their behaviour is essentially natural, truthfully expressing what is experienced within. The behaviour of 'men appassionate' served as a model in the same way; here, too, the orator must avoid 'the excess and exorbitant levity, and keep the manner corrected with prudent mediocrity'.[1]

Anyone who reads *Chirologia* and *Chironomia* must notice how often Bulwer declares that a particular gesture is 'natural to those' who are expressing a particular emotion or who are striving to achieve a particular purpose. He usually quotes from the Bible or the Classics, or from any work of the remote or recent past in order to demonstrate that 'actions' used in his day were also known before it. But his main interest lies in 'action' as the natural expression of emotions and intentions shared by human beings as a whole. He sometimes has no example to give from the writings of the past; then he reminds us that if a gesture is to be seen in daily life around him, that is enough to justify its inclusion in his work. 'Though I annex no example of this gesture, yet the validity thereof is not much the less; and when all is done, somewhat must be left to observation.' This concerns 'the raising up and bowing the fore-finger from us'—a gesture 'natural to those who beckon a retreat or forbid'.[2] Another 'Magistral notion' of his own, so far as he knew, was the account of a gesture suitable to 'advance their utterance, who in discourse touch and handle a matter lightly'. It consists of extending the third finger out of the open hand as if to touch something. Knowing Galen to have said that this finger was used to touch anything lightly, and realizing that the physicians of antiquity had stirred their cordials with it, Bulwer was induced upon this 'ground of nature' to cast 'my mite into the treasury of this art'.[3] A hundred years earlier, Richard Sherry apologized for having 'but briefly touched, and as it were with my little finger pointed

---

[1] Op. cit., pp. 180 ff. [2] *Chirol.*, p. 171.
[3] *Chiron.*, p. 82.

to these things which require a longer declaration'.[1] Bulwer
stresses the need for an 'orator' to observe people, to be aware of
what is going on within them and notice how it is expressed in
their external action. What Philostratus Junior demanded in a
painter is what he requires in an orator: he must be 'a man en-
dued with a good fancy and a sound judgment, actively apt to
everything, and industrious in the observing of men's natures,
and assimilating their manners, and counterfeiting of all things
which in the gesture and composition of the body are the signs
and notes of the tacit mind and affections'.[2]

Chirologia and *Chironomia* are the results not only of Bulwer's
reading and of his knowledge of what was done as 'external
action' by the orator; they contain descriptions of what he saw
done around him by ordinary men and women of all ranks and
callings, and by actors on the stage. Some gestures are lewd,
some are the opposite. Many modern writers on the subject of
Elizabethan acting mistakenly refer to him as a compiler of
descriptions of stereotyped gestures which may have been used
in formal oratory, but have no other relation to the vigour of
real human behaviour or of acting. It is always difficult to take
these writers seriously, as they betray not only an inability to
understand him but in many cases that utter ignorance of what
he says, which suggests that their expert confidence has not
allowed them even to read him. All that they say about him is
amply contradicted by a single gesture, 'vulgarly *Higa*', which
consists of 'the putting forth of the middle finger, the rest drawn
into a fist on each side'; it is 'a natural expression of scorn and
contempt'. Held in this way the hand is fashioned in what Bulwer
calls 'an obscene and filthy manner'.[3] So much for the alleged
academic nature of the 'actions' which he treats. He is equally
in touch with life when he describes the gesture which 'is used
in our nimble-fingered times to call one Cuckold, and to present
the badge of cuckoldry, that mental and imaginary horn; seeming to cry, "O, man of happy note, whom fortune meaning highly

---

[1] *A Treatise of Schemes and Tropes* (1550), sig. A7ᵛ.
[2] *Chiron.*, p. 21.   [3] *Chirol.*, pp. 173, 175.

to promote, hath stuck on thy forehead the earnest-penny of succeeding good luck"'. The gesture is a variant of presenting 'the index and ear finger wagging, with the thumb applied unto the temple'. When the index and ear finger were wagged the gesture was suitable to use towards fools, 'for, this most ridiculous affront implies such men to be asses'. On the stage it was probably used with the blessing upon Bottom who was 'translated'. When the hand was placed to the head in this way, but with the fingers motionless, it was the 'badge of cuckoldry' in real life, and presumably on the stage as well.[1] It seems that Bulwer was wrong in saying that this gesture was the 'badge of cuckoldry' only when the fingers were not wagged. For in 1606, King Christian of Denmark, brother to James I's Queen, gave great offence and caused a deplorable scandal by putting his thumb to his temple and wagging the index and ear fingers when drunk, insulting the aged Earl of Nottingham (the former Lord Howard of Effingham), who had married a young wife three years earlier.[2] No matter how many times Dr. Foakes, Professor Rosenberg, or any other learned writers assure me that Bulwer treats only formal, oratorical gesture, I fear I shall be unable to be persuaded to their point of view so long as I retain a memory of this gesture on this occasion in real life.

Quite the opposite of such profane gestures is that of benediction: 'Both hands modestly extended and erected unto the shoulder points is a proper form of public benediction for the hands of an ecclesiastical orator when he would dismiss his auditors.' This was actually the way in which clergymen pronounced a benediction in real life in the first half of the seventeenth century: 'I never saw any grave or orthodox divine from the pulpit dismissing the people with a blessing, without this adjunct and formal concurrence of the hands.'[3]

I find it hard to believe that anyone who has read Bulwer's account of the following gesture could really believe it to be part

---

[1] *Chirol.*, pp. 181–3.
[2] Folger MS. 6972, pp. 284–5, quoted by G. P. V. Akrigg, *Jacobean Pageant* (1962), p. 81.   [3] *Chiron.*, pp. 59, 63.

of a formal, stereotyped, unnatural art: 'To strike another's palm is the habit and expression of those who plight their troth, give a pledge of faith and fidelity, promise, offer truce, confirm a league, buy, sell, grant covenant, bargain, give or take handsell, engage themselves in suretyship, refer their controversies to an arbiter, put to compromise or choose an umpire, engage themselves to be true and trusty, warrant and assure.' So far from ignoring what people really did in his time, Bulwer has taken note of the way in which this gesture was to be found in daily use around him. He walked among the merchants at the Royal Exchange, 'merely to observe their intercourses of buying and selling'. Anyone who followed his example 'shall soon be satisfied in the natural force of *t*his expression'. But anyone who wanted to see 'the vigour of this gesture in *puris naturalibus* must repair to the Horse Cirque, or Sheep Pens in Smithfield', where he had sometimes been 'in consort with my friend' whom he set 'to observe the pure and natural efforts of these men in the heat of their dealings'.[1]

Another gesture to be observed among Londoners was 'to bring the hand to our mouth and, having kissed it, to throw it from us'. This 'is their expression who would present their service, love and respect to any that are distant from them'. Bulwer had seen people doing this 'at public shows to their friends when their standings have been remote from them'.[2]

Again he describes a practice to be observed in use among his contemporaries 'at this day in judiciary trials and arraignments of noblemen who are tried by their peers'. It consists of laying the hand 'open to our heart, using a kind of bowing gesture' in affirming, swearing, calling upon God to witness a truth. 'When the Lord Steward or Clerk of the Crown asketh the peers whether the nobleman there arraigned be guilty or not, every one of them ceremoniously by his hand to his breast affirms upon his honour and conscience he is, or is not guilty.' It does not seem inconceivable that when their roles demanded such things the actors should have imitated what was done in real life.[3]

---

[1] *Chirol.*, pp. 93, 105.   [2] *Chirol.*, p. 88.   [3] *Chirol.*, pp. 88 f.

ELLEN TERRY
from Pascoe's *Dramatic Notes*, 1882

Bulwer cannot be regarded as a writer of what R. A. Foakes declares manuals of oratory which 'prescribe a formal delivery and use of gesture'.[1] In truth, I have not yet come across any Elizabethan 'manual of oratory' which answers his description; *Chirologia* and *Chironomia* certainly do not, unless we are to agree that to say to wring the hands in sorrow or distress, or to place the forefinger to the lips to indicate the need for silence is to 'prescribe a formal delivery'; or that to stretch out a cupped hand when begging, or shake a clenched fist in rage, or to hold forth the hands as if to be handcuffed are all examples of a formal 'use of gesture'.[2] This last 'action' may strike us as involving a certain amount of formality, simply because today we raise our hands above the head to indicate surrender. It was used, however, by Marius Goring playing Angelo in the 1962 production of *Measure for Measure* at Stratford on Avon, when he submits to the authority of the Duke. Bulwer's *Exprobrabit* may well seem 'formal' to modern eyes (V in Fig. 6): it was used by Ellen Terry as recently as 1882 (see facing plate).

Not the least confusing of the misconceptions held by some people today regarding the relation of the action of the renaissance 'orator' to that of the actor is the belief that the rhetoricians held the stage and its acting in scorn. The truth is exactly the opposite. The Elizabethan 'orator' looked on the player as his master, accepting as true of his own day what was accepted of Greece and Rome, that if it were not for the players the art of rhetorical delivery would itself have languished. In Bulwer we read: 'The art was first formed by rhetoricians; afterwards amplified by poets and cunning motists, skilful in the portraiture of mute poesy: but most strangely enlarged by actors, the ingenious counterfeitors of men's manners.' He names Quintilian as the first Roman orator to collect 'into an art' whatever his experience advised, including 'so much from the theatre to the forum as stood with the gravity of an orator'.[3] Bulwer himself

---

[1] 'The Player's Passion' in *Essays and Studies* (The English Association, 1954), p. 70.
[2] *Chirol.*, pp. 28–29, 168–70, 59–61, 57–59, 41–42.
[3] *Chiron.*, pp. 24 f.

FIG. I

recorded much that was done in his own times in 'schools, theatres and the mansions of the muses'.[1] He is sometimes mistakenly described today as an enemy of the stage, simply because he recognized that some things done by the actors were not suitable to the style and purpose of an orator on a more solemn occasion. As I have pointed out earlier, in doing so he tells us what in fact was done by actors. Moreover he talks of having observed people blowing kisses to one another 'at public shows'. If it be argued that 'public shows' may not mean at theatrical performances, we can still rely on his declaration that the art which he treats was practised in the theatre among other places.

Sir Richard Baker is another who accepted the tradition that the actors in ancient times were responsible for the development of the art, and who regarded the players of his own day as better than the 'orators' in the practice of 'external action'. He is sure 'there never had been so good orators if there had not been first players: seeing the best orators that ever were account it no shame to have learned the gracefulness of their action even from players: Demosthenes from Satyrus; and Cicero from Roscius'.[2] And one of Bulwer's engraved titles shows us Demosthenes, Andronicus, Roscius, and Cicero, all acting. (Fig. 1).

The stage-players offered an even better model than the 'passionate' behaviour of men and women in real life. Actors not only 'let nature work in her kind'; they also showed to perfection the manner 'corrected with prudent mediocrity: this the best may be marked in stage-players, who act excellently; for as the perfection of their exercise consisteth in imitation of others, so they that imitate best, act best'.[3]

Shakespeare's Hamlet agrees. Where Wright says 'leave the excess and exorbitant levity or other defects, and keep the manner corrected with prudent mediocrity', the Prince impresses on his players: 'in the very torrent, tempest, and, as I may say, whirlwind of your passion, you must acquire and beget a temperance that may give it smoothness'. To imitate well was one

---

[1] *Chiron.*, sig. A6ʳ. [2] Op. cit., p. 35.
[3] Wright, op. cit., p. 179.

of the elements of 'action' which was 'commendable in the grave orator'. It was best to 'be marked in stage-players'. What was merely 'commendable' in the orator was 'most exquisitely perfect' in the Elizabethan actor.

Wright says: 'In the substance of external action for most part orators and stage-players agree.'[1] Bulwer supports this when he declares that the gestures of which he gives descriptions are to be seen every day in contemporary life, in the theatres among other places. One 'action' which he treats was not only a feature of real life but obviously was used on the stage: 'And if we see one bite his thumb at us we soon infer he means us no good.'[2] Shakespeare and his players (and presumably their audiences) must have made the same sort of inference when in the first scene of *Romeo and Juliet* Samson declared on an Elizabethan stage: 'I will bite my thumb at them, which is a disgrace to them if they bear it' (I. i. 41–42).

Bulwer relates that he 'lately observed in some at the public taking of the last National Covenant' that they took the oath with both hands held in the way in which it is usual to hold up the right hand today. He felt that they did so rather 'out of a zealous earnestness to engage themselves in the Cause, than out of any affectation'. He remarks that 'to extend and raise up both the hands to heaven' is an expression of 'a most strong kind of asseveration, implying as it were a double oath'.[3] Here again stage practice agreed with rhetorical delivery and the actual behaviour of people in real life. In *The Maid's Tragedy* Melantius orders Evadne:

> Give me thy hands,
> And, both to Heaven held up, swear
> (IV. i. 164–5.)[4]

Quintilian is referred to as Bulwer's ultimate authority for the admonition: 'to use the action of one that saws or cuts' is 'prevaricant in rhetoric'. This was true of stage-playing as well, if we are to give credence to Hamlet's 'Nor do not saw the air too

---

[1] Wright, op. cit., p. 179.   [2] *Chirol.*, p. 160.   [3] *Chirol.*, pp. 52, 51.
[4] Ed. Brooke and Paradise, op. cit., p. 783.

much with the hand thus'. In each case we should read 'saw' in its Elizabethan sense of 'slash'. Quintilian actually augments his account of defective speakers with the statement: 'Solet esse et pigra et trepida et secanti similis'—'There are others, again, whose hands are sluggish or tremulous or inclined to slash the air.'[1]

So much attention was given to Quintilian and 'external action' in the Elizabethan school and university that it is quite likely that Bulwer and Shakespeare and many others knew him as the source of a warning which they must have heard innumerable times. This is an element of external action in which orators and stage-players agreed. For the Elizabethan actor as for the orator to 'saw the air' was to act badly.

Another point which Hamlet makes is also made by renaissance writers on the 'external action' of orators. We read in one manuscript: 'The general rule is, that the gesture be correspondent to the ordering of the voice.'[2] Abraham Fraunce says that gesture 'must follow the change and variety of the voice, answering thereunto in every respect'.[3] From Bulwer we learn: 'Take care that variety of gesture may answer the variety of voice and words.' And: 'Gesture must attend upon every flexion of the voice.'[4] In grammar and song schools all over the country, boys were taught to 'pronounce openly, finely and distinctly, keeping due decorum both with body and with mouth'.[5] The 1541 charter of King's School, Canterbury, where Christopher Marlowe was a pupil, enjoins that the boys shall be taught 'due decorum both with their body and their mouth'.[6]

Here was another reason for acting plays at school and university. Thomas Heywood reminds his reader that acting 'not only emboldens a scholar to speak, but instructs him to speak well'. In particular: 'It instructs him to fit his phrases to his action,

---

[1] *Chiron.*, pp. 102 f.; Quintilian, ed. cit., iv. 306–7.
[2] MS. Ashmole 768, p. 541.
[3] *The Arcadian Rhetoric* (1588), ed. E. Seaton (1950), p. 120.
[4] *Chiron.*, pp. 138, 133.
[5] A. F. Leach, *Documents Illustrating Early Education in Worcester* (1913), pp. 132, 145.   [6] A. F. Leach, *Educational Charters* (1909), p. 467.

and his action to his phrase, and his pronunciation to them both.'[1]
Hamlet says: 'Suit the action to the word, the word to the
action.' The player who obeyed was in agreement with the
'orator' who accepted Bulwer's insistence: 'Nature exhorts all
men to action consentaneous to the style of their elocution.'[2]
The orator suited 'the action to the word' and the actor answered
Nature's exhortation 'to action consentaneous to the style of'
his dramatist's 'elocution'. In Bulwer's day 'elocution' still had
the sense of 'selection and use of words'. It still referred to the
words themselves and not, as today, to the speaking of them.

With both actor and orator, action was the result of allowing
truly felt emotion to communicate itself through trained voice,
facial expression, and movement. Where they differed was as a
result of their respective purposes and functions. The actor read
his author's words to find from them what the character had
been imagined thinking, feeling, and wanting. Evoking within
himself the requisite thought, emotion, and desire, he then had
to express these while articulating the words with which his
dramatist had provided him. But the orator used his own words
to express what he thought, felt, and wanted in his own person,
because he was who he was, and not because he represented a
character in a fiction. He did not have to evoke something
within himself in order to act that character. But like the actor,
the orator needed to feel; and from his feeling, too, he derived
his 'action'.

In Shakespeare's day the difference as well as the similarity
between the two was fully understood. Wright says that they
'only differ in this, that these act feignedly, those really'. The
orators, 'those' who act 'really', express in action truly felt
emotion to attain objectives by stirring up 'all sorts of passions
according to the exigencies of the matter'. But 'these', the players,
who act 'feignedly', use their action to communicate what they
are experiencing within in order to represent an imaginary
person, 'only to delight'.[3]

[1] *An Apology for Actors* (1612), sig. C4ʳ.
[2] *Chiron.*, p. 20.   [3] Op. cit., p. 179.

It was advisable for orators in Elizabethan England to learn from the perfection of the players in the art of external action 'for most part'. But some of the things done on the stage should not be copied; orators had to use 'all gravity, grace, and authority to persuade'. The speaker off the stage should avoid some of the practices of the actors, who 'intermingle much levity in their action to make men laugh'.[1] By describing some of the things which should be avoided, Bulwer and others have left us an account of what in fact the players did.

Clapping of the hands was not for the orator; this was 'fitter for the stage'; it was 'too theatrically light for the hands of any prudent rhetorician'.[2] That this was stage practice is confirmed by the interlude *Jacob and Esau* (c. 1557) with its stage-direction: 'Mido cometh in clapping his hands and laughing.'[3] 'The trembling hand' was wrong for orators; it was 'scenical', belonging 'more to the theatre than the forum'. Where an orator ought never to strike his breast 'with an audible stroke', an actor on the stage would give himself this 'vehement percussion' to communicate the emotion experienced within. To express 'dolour, shame and admiration [i.e. wonder]', actors would strike the forehead with the hand; they did not restrict themselves to the 'bent-in-hand' when beckoning on the stage, but would 'revoke and bow back their whole body, and wind and wrest about their very sides'.[4] Amateurs at school and university might come to a halt on the stage when speaking, so it seems from *The Return from Parnassus*, where Kemp agrees with Burbage that the university actors had 'oftentimes a good conceit in a part', but finds it amusing 'to see them never speak in their walk, but at the end of the stage'.[5] The inference to be drawn here is that the professional actors certainly spoke 'in their walk'.

The evidence which has been considered up to this point suggests that we can use accounts of the 'external action' of the renaissance orators in order to learn more about the 'external

---

[1] Ibid.   [2] *Chiron.*, pp. 105–7. See also Fraunce, ed. Seaton, p. 127.
[3] Act II, Sc. iii, ed. Crowe and Wilson, *Malone Soc. Reprints* (1956), sig. C3ʳ.
[4] *Chiron.*, pp. 104; 46–47; 47; 40–41.
[5] Act IV, Sc. iii, ed. Leishman, *The Three Parnassus Plays* (1949), pp. 336 f.

action' of the players; in 'substance' the two agreed 'for most part'. We have seen that for the lesser part they disagreed in that the orator must be grave, and that the actor communicates emotion which he feels as the result of what Stanislavski calls the magic 'if';[1] the actor imagines what it would be like 'if' he were the imaginary character; then he feels as if he were, so that a by-stander such as Hamlet may remark

> What's Hecuba to him, or he to Hecuba,
> That he should weep for her?

But in each case the acting had to be 'lively' and 'natural'. In each case what was experienced within had to come to truthful expression in voice, face, and gesture. And in each case the artlessness of actual behaviour had to be heightened into art without losing its intensity and truthfulness.

It is misleading to suggest that 'In the intellectual atmosphere of which rhetoric was part, we can discern several attitudes that probably shaped acting.' For the truth is just the opposite: in fact, the acting of the player shaped that of the rhetorician. It is equally erroneous to suggest that 'Rhetorical theory was con-ducive to the growth of formal and traditional acting.'[2] Rhetorical theory insists on natural and lively acting; it insists that emotion must be truthfully felt and naturally expressed; it insists, too, that the best models will be found among the players, for 'Those who imitate best, act best.' The value of a careful and under-standing study of the 'external action' of the Elizabethan 'orator' lies in what is to be learnt about the 'most part' in which it agreed with that of the player. We learn how Elizabethans were able to write, read, and act dramatic texts in which character and unrealistic literature are one; how the player was able to seem to be the very person he represented without his truth and reality clashing with the unrealistic words used by the dramatist, whether they were rhyme, blank verse, or prose, even when, as in *King Lear*, all three are used in the very same scene.

---

[1] See *Stanislavsky on The Art of the Stage*, translated with an Introductory Essay by David Margarschack (1961), pp. 33–44.

[2] B. Beckermann, *Shakespeare at the Globe (1599–1609)* (1962), pp. 120 f.

CHAPTER TWO

The Ingeniousness of the Speech when it is fitted to the Person

WHEN Romeo tells Juliet that he must leave because day is about to break, he uses words which the Elizabethan actor spoke while playing the role 'to the life' so that 'men think it not a play'. His truth and intensity made him seem to be Romeo come to life. But whatever the details of his 'external action' may have been, whatever was done with voice, face, and gesture, he spoke lines which Romeo would not have used. And there was no attempt to suggest that they were not the premeditated words of the author:

> It was the lark, the herald of the morn,
> No nightingale. Look, love, what envious streaks
> Do lace the severing clouds in yonder east;
> Night's candles are burnt out, and jocund day
> Stands tip-toe on the misty mountain tops.
> I must be gone and live, or stay and die.

A real Romeo would not have said 'the herald of the morn'. He would have said in Elizabethan colloquial speech the equivalent of something such as: 'That's the lark, I tell you, it always sings just before dawn—it will be light any minute now.' But with 'the herald of the morn', Shakespeare's imagined Romeo expresses the same thought, emotion, and desire, just as fully and truthfully as the colloquial speech which 'the very man' would have used.

To speak these words so as to communicate truthfully and completely what they express for the character, and at the same time allow their relationship to one another to become apparent

as part of a work of art, is a task which usually baffles the modern
actor. But Shakespeare's actor was equal to it. How he was able
to accomplish this dual task is clearly explained in Elizabethan
accounts of that 'most part' in which there was agreement between the external action of orator and stage-player.

At school boys were taught to be 'lively' and 'natural' in their
'pronunciation and gesture', when they were speaking lines
written by somebody else, as when they spoke their own words.
Learning Latin from dialogues, they were 'to utter every dialogue
lively, as if they themselves were the persons which did speak'.[1]
Whatever was spoken, the general aim was that the boys 'may
do everything according to the very nature'.

They could do this only when understanding the sense of
every word, and the purpose for which it had been used by the
author in a specific context with other words. Meaning decided
how a word was spoken. The voice was inflected 'in single words,
that every one have his intention according to his signification'.
This enabled the tropes and figures through which the writer
was expressing himself to have their effect upon the listener.
Inflexion which conveyed 'intention according to his signification'
was essential so that 'the kinds of tropes (if they be of force) may
appear. For no otherwise can an irony, and a metaphor be made
more manifest and set forth more effectual'.[2] Abraham Fraunce
observes similarly: 'In the particular applying of the voice to
several [i.e. individual] words, we make tropes that be most
excellent plainly appear.' He adds that 'without this change of
voice, neither any irony, nor lively metaphor can well be dis-
cerned'.[3]

One reason for teaching boys to recognize tropes and figures
was that they should be able to speak 'naturally' and 'lively'.
'Let them also be taught carefully in which word the emphasis
lyeth', is Brinsley's advice. This was put on 'those words in
which the chief trope or figure is'.[4] The result was that these
words stood out in the speaking, differentiated from the other

---

[1] Brinsley, op. cit., pp. 212–14.   [2] MS. Ashmole 768, p. 540.
[3] Op. cit., p. 106.   [4] Op. cit., p. 214.

words, but in such a way that the relationship of each to all was apparent to the listener, both as sound and meaning.

A boy taught in this way recognized 'herald' as the word 'in which the chief trope . . . is'. The trope in this case is the metaphor, 'herald of the morn'. The ability to recognize this came only from understanding the basic sense of the words and what they mean in this context. When the speaker imagined himself 'to have occasion to utter the very same things', he spoke 'naturally' and 'lively', and made the metaphor function for his audience. The Elizabethan trained to respond mentally, physically, and vocally in this way spoke 'herald' with an emphasis which communicated what it means for Romeo; it is the bird which sings to announce the imminent arrival of dawn, it gives a warning which is unwelcome, but which must be heeded.

Men and boys who had been taught 'every trope, every figure, as well of words as of sentence' were able to handle verse in this way. Kempe, the schoolmaster, who insisted on such teaching, also declared that the pupils should learn 'the rhetorical pronunciation and gesture fit for every word, sentence and affection'.[1] This does not mean a system of stereotyped gestures, each fitted to a particular trope or figure. The speaker had to imagine himself with 'occasion' to speak the words, with a need to express what is said by them. Then the 'rhetorical pronunciation and gesture' was a combination of vocal inflexion, facial expression, and use of the body which communicated 'naturally' what was within. The speaker's 'function' was determined by what he had to communicate. He was aware of 'herald' as the key word of the metaphor; he was also aware that the trope as a whole means for Romeo that the singing announces daylight, with everything else that is involved as thought, feeling, and desire.

'Whatsoever' might be found 'commendable' in the orator acting Romeo in this way would be excelled when it was performed by the actor; in him it would be 'most exquisitely perfect'. He was better trained in every way, but particularly in identifying himself—'they that imitate best, act best'. He was

---

[1] W. Kempe, *The Education of Children* (1588), sig. G3ʳ.

better at imagining himself to be the person speaking in the play, with the result that his 'applying' of his better-trained voice was more effective. More effective in two ways; first, because it was better trained, with greater range and resonance, being more skilfully produced; second, because it was the instrument of a more complete identification, a more precise and accurate response to the words. This was also true of gesture and face; the action suited the word. Voice, face, and gesture not only made 'tropes that be most excellent plainly appear', but communicated what was going on within the actor as if he had been 'the very man'.

By a 'change of voice' which communicated in articulate sound what was experienced by the actor, he was able to emphasize 'wing', the keyword of the metonymy, by means of which Edgar makes Gloucester believe that they are standing on the edge of a cliff so high that 'the crows and choughs that wing the mid-way air' seem hardly as big as beetles. The actor's voice changed on 'wing' because he used it to convey what happened within him as he imagined himself looking down on the birds from so great a height with as much again between them and the ground as between him and them. The same principle applied to Vendice's 'the smallest advantage *fattens* wronged men',[1] and to Monticelso's reference to Prince Giovanni as 'a *casket*/ For both your crowns'.[2]

What was taught to the orator was equally relevant to the Elizabethan actor's playing of Romeo's bitter:

I must be gone and live, or stay and die.

This involves two examples of the figure of words, antithesis; they were obvious to the Elizabethan reader, and made 'more manifest' by the actor's pronunciation to the eyes and ears of the Elizabethan audience. For what was taught to orators concerned the recognizing and pronouncing not of tropes alone, but of 'every figure, as well of words as of sentence'. Shakespeare's

[1] C. Tourneur, *The Revenger's Tragedy* (1607), ed. J. A. Symonds (1948), I. i, p. 346.
[2] J. Webster, *The White Devil* (1612), ed. J. A. Symonds (1948), II. i, p. 25.

actor understood the line as one in which the relation between
'gone–stay' and 'live–die' expressed a conflict of thought, emotion, and desire within Romeo. The conflict was made 'manifest'
in the inflexion of his voice; the figures were heard not as a
mechanical inflexion, but as the natural and inevitable vocal
result of his experiencing and communicating what they express.
Simultaneously, face and body responded, showing in 'external
action' what was going on within. Shakespeare's unrealistic
words were performed as a combination of articulate sound and
'significant action', at one and the same time a rendering of the
verse as it ought to be rendered and a communication of what
Shakespeare had imagined within Romeo, as if the actor 'were
the man personated'.

It was 'commendable in the grave orator' to treat figures of
words in this way, which was 'exquisitely perfect in' the actor.
What was taught at school in accordance with Latin text-books
is reproduced in the English of Abraham Fraunce's *The Arcadian
Rhetoric*. He describes figures of words as those which 'altogether
consist in sweet repetitions and dimensions.' Antithesis is a figure
consisting in 'dimensions'; rhyme, alliteration, and assonance
depend upon repetition. In pronouncing such figures, says
Fraunce, 'is chiefly conversant that pleasant and delicate tuning
of the voice which resembleth the consent and harmony of some
well ordered song'.[1]

Some figures of words are patterns of articulate sound and
result from the inflexion of voice to convey meaning. Antithesis
belongs to this group. It is to be found in the verse and prose—
dramatic and non-dramatic—of innumerable pieces of Elizabethan
writing. Reading these figures aloud, or acting them in drama,
when the Elizabethan communicated their meaning, his inflexion
made 'more manifest' the connexion between contrasting ideas
and emotions as a relationship of articulate sound.

Puttenham describes antithesis as 'very pleasant and fit for
amplification, which to answer the Greek term, we may call
the encounter, but following the Latin name by reason of his

[1] Ed. Seaton (1950), p. 107.

contentious nature, we may call him the Quarreller, for so be all such persons as delight in taking the contrary part of whatsoever shall be spoken'. He gives these examples of the use of the figure:

> *Good* have I done you, *much*, *harm* did I never *none*,
> *Ready* to *joy* your *gains*, your *losses* to *bemoan*,
> Why therefore should you *grudge* so sore at my *welfare:*
> Who *only bred your bliss*, and *never caus'd your care*.[1]

The Elizabethan responded to this with an awareness of the related ideas expressed in related words. Some of these relations here have been indicated by the use of italics. In addition to these the Elizabethan would have observed the contrast between the 'I' of the poet and the 'you' whom he addresses, with the related contrast of 'your' to 'my'. His speaking would render these things as relationships of articulate sound; it would also express the balance of 'have I done—did I never'.

It is possible to regard this passage as nothing more than an exercise in the use of the figure; nevertheless the patterns are not entirely ends in themselves; the writer has been able to express himself in them fully and precisely. What he expressed could be communicated by the speaker who then sounded natural, as if 'he had occasion to say the very same thing'.

The same mental attitude and the same physical techniques of voice, face, and gesture went into an actor's playing of the prose of Lyly's Eumenides:

> Ay, but if *all virtuous ladies* should yield to *all that be loving*, or *all amiable gentlewomen* entertain *all that be amorous*, their *virtues* would be accounted *vices*, and their *beauties deformities*; for that love can be but between two, and not proceeding of him that is *most faithful*, but *most fortunate*.   (III. iv. 80–86.)[2]

I have called attention elsewhere[3] to the speech in the third

---

[1] *The Art of English Poesy* (1589), ed. G. D. Willcock and A. Walker (1936), p. 210.
[2] J. Lyly, *Endymion* (1591), ed. Brooke and Paradise, p. 53.
[3] *Acting Shakespeare* (1960), pp. 37 f.

act of *The Tempest* in which Ferdinand expresses eleven sets of contrasting ideas:

> There be some *sports* are *painful*, and *their labour*
> *Delight in them* sets off; some kinds of *baseness*
> Are *nobly* undergone, and most *poor matters*
> Point to *rich ends*. This my mean task
> Would be as *heavy* to me as *odious*, but
> The *mistress* which I serve *quickens what's dead*
> And makes my *labours pleasures*. O, *she is*
> *Ten times more gentle* than *her father's crabb'd*
> And he's composed of harshness.
>
> (III. i. 1–9.)

Antithesis became one of the favourite figures of words of English Augustan poets. Their preference probably derived from the same sort of classical education as led to the figure's so frequent appearance in the drama as well as the non-dramatic writing of the Elizabethans. The actor made the figure manifest wherever it occurred. It is obvious in the lines which Thomas Heywood gave to Chester:

> I'll have *full light*, or *none*; *either soar high*,
> *Or else sink low.*

Lady Mary is more complex in the same play:

> *Diamonds*, though *set in lead*, *retain* their *worth*,
> And *leaden knives* may have a *golden sheath*.[1]

Hamlet speaks what is probably one of the best-known examples in English, even if it is not consciously recognized as a figure of words: 'A little *more* than kin and *less* than kind.' The complexity of this utterance derives from the pun, *kin–kind*; the antithetical balances produces much the same rhythm as that of Mistress Anne's 'In this *one life*, I die *ten thousand deaths*' (IV.v. 92).[2] The mind of the Elizabethan actor had been trained to perceive, and his 'external action' to communicate the contrasting ideas in

---

[1] *The Royal King and the Loyal Subject* (1637), ed. J. P. Collier (1850), I. i, p. 7, and II. ii, p. 24.

[2] T. Heywood, *A Woman Killed with Kindness* (1617), ed. Brooke and Paradise, p. 316.

Tamyra's 'All *bars* made *engines* to his insolent fury'.[1] The voice uttered *bars* and *engines* in a way which expressed the character's resentment that what ought to have impeded her adversary had been converted into an instrument to give his will effect.

This attitude to drama meant that the competent actor did not permit himself to ignore the antithetical structure of these lines from Tamburlaine's lament for his dying wife:

> *Now* are those spheres where *Cupid us'd to sit,*
> *Wounding the world* with *wonder* and with *love,*
> Sadly *supplied* with *pale and ghastly death,*
> Whose *darts* do *pierce* the *centre of my soul.*
>
> (II. iii. 3049–52.)[2]

The actor's inflexions made manifest the relationships, 'Now . . . sadly supplied'—'us'd to sit'; 'where Cupid'—'with pale and ghastly death'; 'wounding . . . with wonder and with love'—'whose darts do pierce'; 'the world'—'the very centre of my soul'. He communicated the sense that the spheres where Cupid used to sit are now the spheres where his place is taken up by pale and ghastly death; Cupid wounded the world with wonder and with love, but death's darts pierce the centre of Tamburlaine's soul. On the stage, all the complexities of the sense and its implications—what is thought explicitly and by implication, what is felt and what is wanted—were communicated in 'external action'.

Training in recognizing and applying the voice to 'sweet repetitions' meant that the Elizabethan responded, and made his listener respond, to the pattern in Sidney's sonnet both as a figure of words and as an expression of thought, emotion, and desire:

> Loving in truth, and fain in verse my love to show,
> That the dear she might take some *pleasure* of my *pain,*
> *Pleasure* might cause her *read, reading* might make her *know,*
> *Knowledge* might *pity* win, and *pity grace* obtain.[3]

---

[1] G. Chapman, *Bussy d'Ambois* (1607) (II. ii. 41) ed. Brooke and Paradise (1933), p. 336.

[2] C. Marlowe, *Tamburlaine the Great, Part II* (1590), ed. Tucker Brooke (1929), p. 95.

[3] *Astrophel and Stella* (1591), ed. G. Bullett, *Silver Poets of the Sixteenth Century* (1947), p. 173.

At this moment we are not concerned with the four occurrences of 'might' in these lines, but with the progress from the avowal of pain to the hope of the grace that will heal it. This is the figure of climax which Fraunce defines as 'a reduplication continued by diverse degrees and steps, as it were, of the same word or sound'.[1] The boy acting Rosalind in the Elizabethan theatre was confronted with this pattern in Shakespeare's dramatic prose:

For your brother and my sister no sooner *met* but they *look'd*; no sooner *look'd* but they *lov'd*; no sooner *lov'd* but they *sigh'd*; no sooner *sigh'd* but they *ask'd* one another *the reason*; no sooner knew *the reason* but they sought *the remedy*—and in these degrees have they made a pair of stairs to marriage, which they will climb incontinent, or else be incontinent before marriage.

(*As You Like It*, v. ii. 30–36.)

Shakespeare obviously knew that he was using the figure of climax—'a pair of stairs', 'in these degrees'. Puttenham also speaks of this figure as a ladder: he remarks that it 'may be called the marching figure, for after the first step all the rest proceed by double the space, and so in our speech one word proceeds double to the first that was spoken'. He gives this example:

His *virtue* made him *wise*, his *wisdom* brought him *wealth*,
His *wealth* won many *friends*, his *friends* made much *supply*.

We are told 'it may as well be called the *climbing* figure, for *Climax* is as much as to say as a ladder', especially in this example which shows 'how a very mean man by his wisdom and good fortune came to a great estate and dignity'.[2]

There is a superb example of this figure in Book Two of Spenser's *Faerie Queene*:

all that pleasing is to living ear,
Was there consorted in one harmony,
Birds, voices, instruments, winds, waters, all agree.

---

[1] Op. cit., p. 38.   [2] Op. cit., pp. 207 f.
811606   D

The joyous *birds* shrouded in cheerful shade,
Their notes unto the *voice* attempred sweet;
Th' angelical soft trembling *voices* made
To th' *instruments* divine respondence meet:
The silver sounding *instruments* did meet
With the base murmur of the *water's fall*:
The *water's fall* with difference discreet,
Now soft, now loud, unto the *wind* did call:
The gentle warbling *wind* low answered to all.
(Canto xii, lxx, lxxi.)[1]

The difference between speaking non-dramatic passages and passages of dialogue or monologue when climax is involved was determined by the respective differences between what is expressed by the words. With Spenser as with Shakespeare the Elizabethan's voice made the figure manifest; with Spenser the articulate sound merely communicated the description as that has been imagined by the author, but with Shakespeare there was communication of the thought, emotion, and wish of the character imagined speaking these lines. Shakespeare's pattern was heard in Rosalind's voice because the boy used it to express her emotions as she recounted how these two fortunate lovers have fallen in love at first sight, unimpeded by the obstacles which separate her and Orlando, two who also fell in love at first sight, but the course of whose love has been less smooth. As Rosalind speaks she is longing for Orlando to pierce her disguise and recognize his true love in the boy, Ganymede.

Sir Richard Baker remarks that the Elizabethan playgoer drew his 'contentment' from this fusion of a rendering of the dramatist's art with words with a lively, natural representation of the character. The satisfaction was derived from 'the ingeniousness of the speech when it is fitted to the person'.[2] Spenser has 'ingeniousness of speech', but he does not fit it to a person. In drama, however, speech is both ingenious and appropriate to the character. The Elizabethan actor sounded natural because he

---

[1] Ed. J. C. Smith (1961), i. 337.
[2] *Theatrum Triumphans* (1670), pp. 34 f.

gave to each of the key-words of the climax those qualities of tone which enabled him to communicate what they express of the character's thought, feeling, and wish to obtain an objective: this held good when he played Claudius announcing his intention of celebrating Hamlet's triumph:

> Let the kettle to the *trumpet* speak,
> The *trumpet* to the *cannoneer* without,
> The *cannons* to the *heavens*, the *heaven* to earth,
> Now the King drinks to Hamlet.
>
> (v. ii. 267–70.)

The First Knight demanded this same treatment when the actor declared in his person:

> From *naught* at first, thou cam'st to *little* wealth
> From *little* unto *more*, from *more* to *most*.
>
> (I. ii. 338–9.)[1]

And whoever played the Viceroy in *The Spanish Tragedy* applied his voice to make the figure 'more manifest' as he represented with truth and intensity the self-reproach and sorrow with which the disastrous chain of circumstances is recalled, which led from a breach of faith to the loss of a beloved child:

> My late ambition hath distain'd my *faith*;
> My breach of *faith* occasion'd *bloody wars*:
> Those *bloody wars* have spent my *treasure*;
> And with my *treasure* my people's *blood*;
> And with their *blood*, my joy and *best belov'd*,
> My *best belov'd*, my sweet and only son.
>
> (I. iii. 33–38.)[2]

The same principle applied to rhyme. The actor and his audience experienced Richard II's lines as a couplet, a product of art that did not pretend to be other than it was. York has just warned him against injustice which will

> prick my tender patience to those thoughts
> Which honour and allegiance cannot think.

---

[1] C. Marlowe, *The Jew of Malta*, ed. Tucker Brooke, p. 250.
[2] Ed. Brooke and Paradise (1933), p. 103.

To which Richard's reply is:

> Think what you will, we seize into our hands
> His plate, his goods, his money, and his lands.
>
> (II. i. 207–10.)

The ingeniousness of the speech did not suffer in the actor's treatment. Where Shakespeare has fitted that ingeniousness to the person, the acting followed suit. Richard's arrogant self-confidence, his resentment of his relations, his need of money, his selfishness and his enjoyment of his elegance and triumph, were truthfully and naturally expressed in a performance of 'external action' in which every figure of words was given the 'rhetorical pronunciation and gesture' which it required. In this case the result was an actor who seemed to be the very man while he made the figure manifest: without truthful acting, the figure of rhyme could not be effective; without the figure of rhyme being spoken effectively, the representation could not be truthful. The ingeniousness of the Elizabethan author's speech sometimes gave a character rhyme in which to utter a *sententia* which has some bearing upon the play as a whole or upon some part of its action. Thus Bosola, beside the body of the strangled Duchess, recognizes:

> While with vain hopes our faculties we tire,
> We seem to sweat in ice and freeze in fire.[1]

The actor rhymed 'tire' and 'fire' as the result of needing the words to express his disillusion, his realization of so much frantic endeavour senselessly and uselessly misapplied, his sense of guilt for the sins committed and wantonly, uselessly, committed. Where rhyme has been used to give polish and round off a scene or act as it comes to an end, or to serve the same purpose as a speaker leaves the stage in the midst of a scene, the Elizabethan fused in his acting the two elements, character and literature, as inseparably as they are fused in the author's text.

---

[1] J. Webster, *The Duchess of Malfi* (1623), ed. J. A. Symonds (1948), IV. ii. p. 214.

In *A Woman Killed With Kindness*, Frankford resigns himself to his troubles as the will of God:

> But He that *made us, made us* to this woe.
>
> (v. v. 34)

This is the figure of words to which Puttenham gives the title 'the Underlay, or Cuckoo-spell'. A more formal name for it is Epizeuxis. Puttenham's example is hardly more than mechanical repetition for the sake of the pattern:

> The chiefest staff of mine assured stay,
> With no small grief *is gone, is gone* away.[1]

But the ruefulness of Sidney's line from Sonnet XXXIII is aptly expressed in the figure:

> But to *my self, my self* did give the blow.

Other examples are to be found in Shakespeare. Nestor declares:

> —why, then the thing of courage,
> As roused *with rage, with rage* doth sympathize.
>
> (*Troilus and Cressida*, I. iii. 51–52.)

The figure is used when Lucius remarks how aptly the disguised Imogen has been named:

> Thy name well fits *thy faith, thy faith* thy name.
>
> (*Cymbeline*, IV. ii. 384.)

I have given elsewhere a detailed account of figures of words as they are treated in Elizabethan rhetoric books and used in non-dramatic prose and verse and in Shakespeare.[2] Nevertheless it is worth taking this opportunity of calling attention again to the felicity of Elizabethan playwrights in creating character in terms of 'ingeniousness' of language. Thanks to the training to which we are introduced in the treatments of the external action of the 'orator', the Elizabethan actor played Henry V so that Shakespeare's figure made its effect as 'ingeniousness of speech'

---

[1] Op. cit., p. 201.   [2] *Acting Shakespeare*, pp. 20 ff.

perfectly fitted to the person. The King emphasizes to the French Ambassador the consequences of the Dauphin's insulting gift of the tun of tennis balls; they will rebound on France as gun-stones, and:

> many a thousand widows
> Shall this his *mock mock* out of their dear husbands;
> *Mock* mothers from their sons, *mock* castles down.

Antanaclasis is the name which the grammar-school boy learnt to give to a repetition of the same word in different senses. Puttenham calls it 'the Rebound' because it works in a way reminiscent of 'the tennis-ball which being smitten with the racket rebounds back again'.[1] To some extent the effect of the figure in the theatre depended upon the listener's ability to identify it with Puttenham's account of it; but much more depended upon the actor's performance of Henry as if he were the very man needing each repetition of *mock* to express what he must at this moment. The figure has not been used by Shakespeare as an end in itself; and so the actor's function was not to use it as such, but to say what he had to in the person of Henry by means of it. This 'rebound' was manifest, not as a pattern isolated from the rest of the lines, but as part of a larger whole, in which every detail communicated the character's thought, his feeling, and what he wants—to wipe out this insult in a way suggested by the original provocation.

Remarking on the presence of figures of this sort in Milton's verse, F. T. Prince very surprisingly suggests Tasso as the poet's model.[2] Milton learnt the use of figures of words partly from the books which he read in school where he had teaching in Butler's *Rhetoric* among others;[3] and partly he learnt how figures are used from reading in the whole of poetry available to him. If grammar school did nothing else it made fairly certain that a man of average sensibility and intelligence would be incapable of

[1] Op. cit., p. 207.
[2] *The Italian Element in Milton's Verse* (1954), pp. 123 ff.
[3] See D. L. Clark, *John Milton at St. Paul's School* (1948), pp. 147 ff.

ignoring the presence of, and the meaning expressed in, the figure
Paronomasia (Puttenham's 'Nicknamer') in Macbeth's:

> and catch
> With his *surcease*, *success*.
> (I. vii. 3–4.)

Henry V combines it with other figures in:

> And some are yet ungotten and unborn
> That shall have *cause* to *curse* the Dauphin's scorn.
> (I. ii. 287–8.)

This figure seems especially fitted to irony and scorn; it allows
Flamineo to reject his mother's reproaches with the aggressive:

> what means have you
> To keep me from the galley or the gallows?
> (*The White Devil*, I. ii.)[1]

The other 'verbal conceits' which Professor Prince finds as
a link between Milton and Tasso were known to the Elizabethan
whether he learnt about them in school, responded to them in
his reading of the poets, or when he heard them from the mouth
of an actor who made them 'manifest' in his acting as an essential
element of his behaviour as if he had occasion to say the very
same things.

Elizabethan schooling gave the same sort of attention to what
Kempe called 'figures of sentence'. Fraunce defines a figure of
sentence as one 'which in the whole sentence' expresses 'some
motion of the mind'. This demanded that the speaker felt truly
the emotion before he could give the figure the emphasis and
action it required. Fraunce says that in figures of the 'affections'
[i.e. figures expressing emotion] the voice was to be 'more
manly' than in figures of words, 'yet diversely according to the
variety of passions that are to be expressed'.[2] The Elizabethan
speaking the climax from *The Faerie Queene* did not have the
same 'manly' quality of tone that was produced when he acted
Claudius' hypocritical anticipation of his pleasure in Hamlet's
victory over Laertes. The attitude to the lines which was

---

[1] Ed. cit., p. 19.   [2] Op. cit., pp. 63, 107.

fostered and trained in 'pronouncing' emotional figures as such developed an ability to communicate fully and truthfully 'the variety of passions' which might be expressed through a figure of words. Fraunce gives English examples of figures which are in Talaeus' 'rules of pronouncing', and which the Elizabethan was more likely to meet at school in Butler's *Rhetoric*.[1]

What was taught to the 'orator' in this field, he could find most competently put into practice by the actor. It might be in speaking Kent's 'Approach, thou beacon to this under globe', which involved a change of voice to communicate the meaning of the metaphor 'beacon'; or it might be in Lady Macbeth's plain invocation, 'Come, you spirits', where again the voice allowed every word 'to have his intention according to his signification' for the character. The actor did in a manner 'most exquisitely perfect' what the orator, for all his striving, was unable to achieve in a manner that was more than 'commendable'. The exercises in school show what each aimed at. When boys spoke Corderius, Aesop, and the plays of Terence, they were directed to speak naturally, imagining themselves personally to be involved and to need the words allotted to them. Brinsley advocates making them act Virgil's *Eclogues* 'yet still more lively in saying without book to express the affections and persons of shepherds; or whose speech soever else they are to imitate'. In addition to such formal exercises as pronouncing the figures of sentence in Butler and Talaeus, they could acquire practice in pronouncing the prosopopeias of Jupiter, Juno, Apollo, and other personages in Ovid's *Metamorphoses* and Virgil's *Aeneid*. The boys were to be made to do it 'to the life' in all authors 'wherein persons are feigned to speak'. Valuable practice came in pronouncing with the correct emphasis (which means the natural one) 'some of Tully's orations, which are most flowing in figures of sentences (especially in exclamations, prosopopeias, apostrophes and the like: as some against Catiline)'.[2]

When the actor was trained to approach his role and play it in this way, he did justice to the words given by Shakespeare to

---

[1] Op. cit., Bk. I, pp. 26 ff. [2] Op. cit., pp. 212–14.

Romeo both as an 'ingenious' use of language, and as a truthful representation of the character's thoughts, feelings, and desires, as if he were the man himself. What he felt as he imagined himself in Romeo's position decided the tone and other elements of emphasis given to make the trope, 'herald of the morn', manifest. He imagined himself seeing the light emerging in the east, where streaks criss-crossed like lacing as if holding together the two segments of darkness. But this lacing does not hold together, it pushes the severing parts further asunder; it seems to begrudge him every minute with Juliet, and sharpens his bitterness at having to leave after so short a time with his wife. It is in order for day to separate illicit lovers, but not a married couple blessed by holy church. Romeo's resentment of the dawn at this moment, together with his reluctance to go, and his need to make Juliet realize that he must leave her, all find expression in two images. First, he insists that this light is daylight, the weak short-burning lights of the night are all extinguished; then he personifies his enemy, day, offensively happy, placing the tips of his toes, just printing the first suggestion of light on the mountain tops which are still concealed by darkness. The actor looked and sounded natural, because he used every word to communicate its 'intention according to its signification' as if he were Romeo, suiting his action to the word. This did not nullify but made 'more manifest' all that there is in 'the ingeniousness' of the author's verse.

It seems reasonable to conjecture that the rhythm of the lines was evoked as a matter of course by the actor who played his role in this way, and that he experienced it physically, and communicated it as an integral element in the rhythm of his acting. The evidence for this conjecture comes solely from what in fact happens today when an actor prepares and performs a Shakespearian role in accordance with the account of Elizabethan acting given in this chapter. The poet's metre, the pattern of stressed and unstressed syllables, is established when each word is given its sense in accordance with Elizabethan usage so far as stress is concerned. But it is impossible to speak all the sense of many lines of Elizabethan dialogue using only stress, which is a per-cussion. In addition the actor must use intonation; he must inflect his voice, changing pitch and length in order to commu-nicate the explicit sense expressed in the lines. The foundation of the rhythm now begins to emerge as a counterpointing of the intonations demanded by sense, inter-weaving with the basic pattern of stressed and unstressed syllables. When the actor imagines himself to be the man he is 'personating', thinking, feeling, and wanting what is implied by the explicit sense of his lines, the rhythm is affected by the resulting changes of pace, the variations in depth and intensity of tone, in volume. The rhythm thus created, like the rest of the verbal music, is the result of the actor behaving as if he had occasion to speak the words, as if he were the character; he creates the rhythm by using every word as it exists in relation to every other word, so that each has its 'intention' according to the 'signification' which it has for the imagined character. This being what happens in fact when a modern actor acts in accordance with Elizabethan direc-tions, it is not unreasonable to conjecture that the Elizabethans produced the rhythm in their acting in the same way. But it must be emphasized that so far as Elizabethan acting is concerned this is no more than conjecture. On the other hand it is an accurate account of what certainly takes place when modern actors approach Elizabethan drama in accordance with Eliza-bethan principles and practice so far as concerns the 'ingenious-ness of the speech when it is fitted to the person' and the playing of the person to whom it is fitted.

Today when an actor plays Elizabethan dialogue in this manner, the result is a satisfactory fusion of the natural with the artificial. His tones are natural to him; they are the ones which he will always use when communicating what the words express for him as thought, emotion, and desire. But while these tones and the stresses, the pauses and changes of pace and volume are all natural, they are natural sounds produced in accordance with an artificial pattern of words. The intonation, stresses, changes of pace and volume are such as the very man would use; but the pattern which these natural elements of speech produce makes its effect as an obvious artifact; the relation between these natural elements of speaking and the pattern which they produce is like that of the relation between the truthful thought, feeling, and desire expressed in 'the herald of the morn' and the metaphor itself. In each case there is a fusion of what the very man would really do with what he would not do if he were to come to life in the given situation.

What has been written here about rhythm in Elizabethan acting must obviously be conjecture, based on what is fact concerning rhythm in acting today. It is much more than conjecture, however, to say that the Elizabethan was aware of his lines as literature and the speech of a character simultaneously. There is evidence to support this: the Elizabethans say that natural speaking is the result of emphasizing the key words of the figures. These exist in the text. It follows then that to emphasize them was to speak naturally in Elizabethan times just as it is to speak naturally today.

The Elizabethan actor did not need anything more than an elementary knowledge of the schemes and tropes. Given the acting ability, the average grammar-school boy knew enough to do justice to the 'ingeniousness of the speech' in which the dramatist expressed what he was imagining within the character. But such elementary knowledge was essential. Thomas Heywood remarks that actors should either know how to speak as scholars, or possess a natural 'volubility', which enables them to speak well when they do not understand what they are speaking. Each of these defects could be corrected by training: the scholar could be taught to speak well and the natural actor to appreciate the 'ingeniousness' of the lines:

Actors should be picked out personable according to the parts they present; they should be rather scholars, that though they cannot speak well, know how to speak; or else to have that volubility that they can speak well, though they understand not what, and so both imperfections may by instructions be helped and amended: but where a good tongue and a good conceit both fail, there can never be a good actor.[1]

[1] *Apology for Actors*, sig. E3^{r}.

Heywood's 'they should be rather scholars' suggests that he preferred recruits of this sort to those of the other. But whichever the newcomer might be, not very much was required to make him 'scholar' enough. I have myself found that it is not difficult to instruct modern actors and acting students in the elementary knowledge of Shakespeare's use of figures and tropes which enables them to grasp how to use his technique of words to penetrate into the depths of character; and then, conversely, how to seem to be the very men in using that verbal technique to communicate what they are experiencing within, by means of voice, face, and movement in 'external action' which is truthful and intense. This experience leads me to assume that what can be done today could have been done much more efficiently in Elizabethan England. It is a fact that the elements of this technique are enough to make an actor competent with Elizabethan verse. Once the Elizabethan had grasped them, his ability to force his soul to his own conceit enabled him to create the character in the author's style. And there is every reason to believe that Elizabethan actors had far more than an elementary knowledge of pronouncing 'ingenious' speeches.

CHAPTER THREE

The Substance of External Action

NOWADAYS, thanks to Stanislavski, it is prudent for a book or course of study on acting to treat inner preparation as well as what might be called the training in external technique. But before Stanislavski it was usual to accept as axiomatic the fact that if an actor was to move others he must first feel himself; writers on the art concentrated on the external details, not because it was thought that nothing else mattered, but apparently because it was too difficult a task to analyse and attempt to teach the inner preparation. It is possible that until the last hundred years, conditions of entry into the theatre and of subsequent training were such that a great deal of what now has to be taught to comparatively mature beginners was handed on as a matter of course to those who began as boys and girls before the pressures of social custom could inhibit them from free creation of character out of the depths of their own respective personalities. Certainly the 'arts of acting' of the seventeenth, eighteenth, and nineteenth centuries abound in descriptions of gestures and attitudes, with accounts of the way in which each individual passion shows itself in a human being's appearance and voice. But this does not mean that the writers regarded the art which they treated as 'formal' in the sense in which that word is used in contradistinction to 'natural' when speaking of acting.[1] At first sight the plates in Gilbert Austin's *Chironomia* (1806) seem to suggest that he had compiled a collection of conventional gestures and ill-advisedly advocated their use, unaware that there is more to acting. But he knew that true feeling was involved, and that the actor had to represent the character as if he were the very man. He has recorded what was actually done

[1] A. Harbage, *A Theatre for Shakespeare* (1955), p. 95.

in his day, by actors as well as public speakers, and includes drawings of Kemble and Sarah Siddons taken from performance. There is plenty of evidence that this brother and sister were each identified when acting: she, in particular, responded when listening silently and kept herself in character when off-stage in a way which would have won from the Elizabethans the praise given to Burbage and the Excellent Actor.[1]

The dispute about acting in which Diderot's name is prominent and which is treated by Archer in *Mask or Face?* (1888), is really a matter of confusion in terms. An actor who really feels emotion and really strives for an objective as if he were the imaginary character may easily speak loosely of feeling himself to be the person he represents. So Garrick seems to have brought on himself Johnson's ridicule; but in fact when he was on the stage Garrick, however completely identified, still knew that he was an actor performing on a stage. Conversely, although John Philip Kemble could please Johnson by confirming that he was not one of those enthusiasts who believed themselves 'transformed into the very character' he represented, it was equally true that in performance he felt and behaved as if he were that man, while knowing that he was not. In preparing a role he identified himself so strongly that Boaden could perceive his dress and behaviour in his own life gradually approximating to those of the character he was studying. Although he and his sister did the things described and illustrated by Austin, their art was not formal; each seemed to be the imaginary person come to life.

Renaissance works on 'external action' concentrate on the same aspects of the art as we find treated by Austin and Garcia.[2] To avoid misinterpreting Bulwer we must bear in mind the fact that his plates of gestures are intended to illustrate what was being done rather than to insist what must be done as a rigid convention. He and other writers on the subject in the Renaissance accepted the axiom that external action, to be truthful and effective, must spring from inner feeling and desire. His

---

[1] See the present writer's *The Tragic Actor* (1959), pp. 208 ff. and 216 ff.
[2] G. Garcia, *The Actors' Art* (1882).

Chironomia and *Chirologia* reveal how an Elizabethan by means of gesture might validly communicate clearly and powerfully, in a poetry of movement, what he was thinking, feeling, and willing to achieve when representing a character in an Elizabethan play. Of course, when an actor trained in this poetry of movement was content with no more than the external fluidity, then the result must have been what Stanislavski would have denounced as 'an external superficial line'. But bodily movement properly expressed what he approves of as 'the projection of some inner experience'. That was the Elizabethans' aim; when they attained it, their gesture was what he calls 'real action with purpose and content'.[1]

It is certain that the 'actions' described by such writers as Bulwer can be used validly and stirringly by modern actors as 'the projection of some inner experience'. Acting students whom I have taught, professional actors whom I have coached and directed, have found in these gestures 'real action with purpose and content' in the manner indicated by Stanislavski.

Members of the Mermaid Theatre cast used gestures described and illustrated by Bulwer when they performed the first scene of *Hamlet* under my direction at St. John's Wood in 1951. As the actors were primarily concerned with projecting an inner experience, the result was that the gestures were, in the words of *The Times*, 'incorporated in a flowing line that seems to arise naturally from the verse'. The critic declares that for this reason 'they are not stilted'.

The gestures incorporated into this flowing line which seemed to arise naturally from the verse included that which Bulwer describes as suitable to an antithesis: 'If both hands by turns behave themselves with equal art, they fitly move to set off any matter that goes by way of antithesis or opposition.'[2] (P in Fig. 5). Horatio used his right hand whenever distinguishing the dead King Hamlet in his mind from old Fortinbras, for whom he used the left. When Bernardo expresses his indignation that

[1] C. Stanislavski, *Building a Character* (1950), pp. 161 f.
[2] *Chiron.*, p. 58.

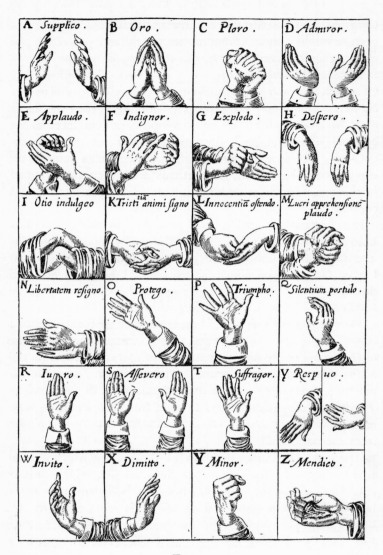

FIG. 2

Horatio should refuse to credit this dreaded sight 'twice seen of us', the actor beat with two fingers of his right hand against the palm of his left. Another of Bulwer's points is that while the hand cannot be used to ask a question, 'yet commonly when we demand, however it be composed, we use to change or turn our hand, raising it a little upwards'.[1] This was done by the actor playing Bernardo as he asked the questions in the passage which begins:

> Why this same strict and most observant watch
> So nightly toils the subject of the land?

I have since been assured by Mr. Miles that what Bulwer says of renaissance external action in this respect still applies to modern acting. 'I've always turned up my hands to give a questioning— so have all actors.'[2]

Playing the Ghost in 1951, Mr. Miles himself used at least two of Bulwer's 'actions'. As he went with martial stalk across the stage his bent-in left hand rested upon his hip in the manner which the Renaissance regarded as unfit for an orator because it was expressive of pride and ostentation: 'To set the arms agambo or aprank, and to rest the turned in back of the hand upon the side, is an action of pride and ostentation, unbeseeming the hand of an orator.'[3] It certainly fitted the hand of a modern actor playing the Ghost walking in the fair and warlike majesty with which the dead King had commanded his troops in life. The hand is often to be seen placed in this way in Elizabethan prints and paintings: it is needed to wear the short Elizabethan cloak with the right air of elegance and assurance. There is every probability that this is how Elizabethan actors bore themselves when playing noble persons on the stage.

Mr. Miles used another action described by Bulwer: 'The two inferior fingers (A in Fig. 6) shut in, and the other three presented in an eminent posture in the extended hand, is a speaking action, significant to demand silence, and procure audience.'[4]

---

[1] *Chiron.*, p. 37.   [2] In a private communication.
[3] *Chiron.*, p. 104.   [4] *Chiron.*, p. 67.

FIG. 3

As Horatio asked his last question, this Ghost, downstage now, actually did what is described later to the Prince:

> It lifted up its head and did address
> Itself to motion like as it would speak.

The arm and hand held in this way allowed the Ghost to dominate the three watchers and the audience. And when the hand came down to go out from the body again, with the actor's mouth starting to open, it seemed as if the cock-crow had really come at the very moment when the apparition was about to speak.

Before our more ambitious production of *Macbeth* in 1952, I wrote that the aim was for the cast to speak 'verse, purely as verse, but without ever making the audience uneasy with people on the stage who sound or look unnatural'.[1] I emphasized the fact that the acting 'must not be stereotyped'; and added that it would 'allow each individual to apply his technique and individuality'. Without attempting an exhaustive analysis of the acting it is possible to mention a few of the gestures included in renaissance treatises on external action which were used by the cast to communicate an inner experience. 'To wring the hands is a natural expression of excessive grief, used by those who condole, bewail and lament.'[2] It consists of pressing the hands together with the fingers interlaced, as if to strain moisture out of an object (*Ploro*, C, Fig. 2). Lady Macbeth's lamentation was communicated in this way as well as in her features and voice as she admitted to herself:

> Nought's had, all's spent,
> Where our desire is got, without content.

And when Lady Macduff asked bitterly, 'Why, then, alas, do I put up that womanly defence?', her wretchedness showed itself in the wringing of her hands. As this wringing is an externalizing of an inner experience of pressure, it was also used by

---

[1] 'Speaking Shakespeare,' *Theatre Newsletter* (1952), vi. 139. 19 f.
[2] *Chirol.*, pp. 28 f.

A. *Inven* *tione* *labo-* *ro*. B. *Fleo*. C. *Approbo*. D. *Extollo*.

E. *Collateraliter* *siro* *moï*. F. *Indico*. G. *Terrorem incutio*. H. *Silen* *indi-* *tiū* *co*.

I. *Redarguo*. K. *Compello*. L. *Veto*. M. *Diffidentia noto*.

N. *Mo* *litiem* *pro* *do*. O. *Conviciū facio*. P. *Contemno*. Q. *Ironiam infligo*.

R. *Contemptuosé* *provoco*. S. *Avariciam prodo*. T. *Offensiunculam* *resentio*. V. *Iram impotentē* *prodo*.

W. *Stultitiæ notam* *infigo*. X. *Improbitatem* *objicio*. Y. *Parco* *Da*. Z. *Numero*.

Fig. 4

one of the witches imagining herself squeezing the shipman dry as she exulted, 'I'll drain him dry as hay'.

Bulwer writes of the gesture, *floccifacit*: 'The middle finger strongly compressed by the thumb, and their collision producing a flurting sound, and the hand so cast out, is an action convenient to slight and undervalue, and to express the vanity of things.'[1] The late Mr. Geoffrey Taylor 'cast out' his hand in this way, when, as Malcolm, he related how nobly the traitor had laid down his life

> As one that had been studied in his death
> To throw away the dearest thing he ow'd
> As 'twere a careless trifle.

Horatio had snapped his fingers in this way in *Hamlet* in 1951, with his infuriating 'Tush, tush, 'twill not appear'.

Bernard Miles found himself expressing Macbeth's emotion truthfully and with intensity, as Macbeth asserts that Duncan's host should ''gainst his murderer shut the door'. He benefited from Bulwer's assertion that 'Both hands objected with the palms adverse, is a foreright adjunct of pronunciation, fit to help the utterance of words coming out in detestation, despite and expro-bation' (*Execratione repellit*, W, Fig. 5). Mr. Miles also incor-porated into his acting the method described as fitting 'their purpose who would number their arguments, and by a visible distinction set them all on a row upon their fingers'.[2] It involves letting the right index finger 'marshal-like go from finger to finger' of the left hand 'to note them with a light touch'. The gesture was a valid externalizing of emotion and purpose as Macbeth taunted the murderers, insisting that the valued file distinguishes

> the swift, the slow, the subtle,
> The house-keeper, the hunter.

According to Wright this was done in real life by 'witty women when they chide', who 'with their fingers number the wrongs

---

[1] *Chiron.*, p. 81. See also *Chirol.*, p. 176.   [2] *Chiron.*, pp. 54, 83.

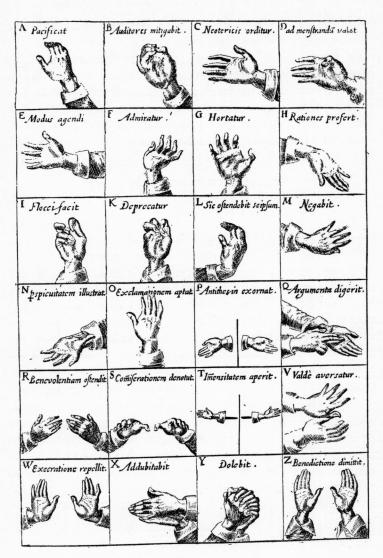

FIG. 5

offered them, the harms, injuries, disgraces and what not thought, said and done against them'.[1]

If we are to judge by the verdict of the dramatic critics, the audience at *Macbeth* in 1952 was never 'uneasy with people on the stage' who looked or sounded unnatural. 'To the lay eye the laboratory-tested Global gestures . . . are remarkably like ours', was the verdict of Eric Keown in *Punch*. He was right, of course; they are exactly the same in many cases; and when they differ, the modern audience is not necessarily aware of anything untowardly archaic. W. A. Darlington wrote that it was not until he read the programme note after all was over 'that I realized I had been witnessing anything so impressively recondite'. Similarly, J. C. Trewin found nothing to worry him—'It seemed perfectly normal'.

But it was not, as Roy Walker, alone of the critics, was acute enough to notice, even while he was responding to the acting primarily as the truthful communication of the actors' experience. Remarking that Bernard Miles and Josephine Wilson avoided 'static poses and scholarly semaphore', he continued:

> Their acting was greatly helped rather than hindered by dramatically significant movement that often communicated a sensation of watching Elizabethan performers and speech that at least invited us to share imaginative and emotional ordeals that were not conceived in the idiom of modern experience. Retrospective analysis can catch Mr. Miles in the stance familiar from old prints, slightly bent forward with one leg advanced and knees flexed, and identify the finger-count, 'the swift, the slow, the subtle, etc.', as a rhetorical figure, but at the time one was primarily aware of the dramatic effect.[2]

All these critics apparently expected 'static poses and scholarly semaphore'; as we see, for instance from the bewildered grumble of *The Spectator* that the acting style was 'scarcely archaic enough to attract attention', despite the fact that he had been witnessing gestures which were used much earlier than Shakespeare's day by Greek and Roman actors and orators. The cast in this

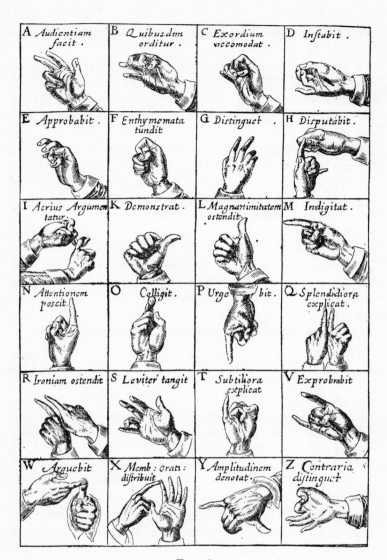

FIG. 6

Macbeth used their 'external action' not to demonstrate gesture to an audience expectant of a novelty, but to carry out what Stanislavski called 'some vital purpose, the projection of some inner experience'. That was why for the most part nothing unusual was noticed when much that was unusual was done.

Mr. Miles gave a perfect example of the transcending of a conventional cliché into 'real action with purpose and content' after his entry, brooding with crossed arms, in the second scene of Act Three. It is well known that this was for the Elizabethans a typical sign of melancholy. Mr. Miles used it to attain an inner reality of what Macbeth calls later being 'cabin'd, cribb'd, confin'd'. But when he came to 'let the frame of things disjoint, both the worlds suffer', the inner reality was one of paramount need to break out of what was restricting him; he strove to attain his objective imaginatively, externalizing the striving in a breaking apart of the knot of his arms, bringing down both clenched fists in a massive determination to destroy anything that might impede him.

It should not surprise us that modern actors are able to make use of 'gestures' described in renaissance works on 'external action'. For, as Bulwer and Wright never tire of reminding their readers, the art aimed at expressing naturally thought, emotion, and purpose natural to human beings. 'Nature assigns to each motion of the mind its proper gesture, countenance and tone, whereby it is significantly expressed',[1] says Bulwer. After all, he is giving us nothing more than an account of what was done in his day supplemented by a history of each gesture with quotations relating to it from the Bible and secular writings of the past. How sound renaissance writers on this subject are is illustrated by what actually happened in a production of *Richard II* in which I assisted Mr. John Hale at the Theatre Royal, Bristol, in 1961. Mr. Jeremy Spenser, playing Aumerle, without having had the action suggested to him, was impelled to stamp his foot in his frustrated rage when this character is accused of treason before the new King, Henry IV. This is what an Elizabethan actor

[1] *Chiron.*, p. 23.

would almost certainly have done. Christopher Johnson, at Winchester, taught his boys when they acted, 'supplosion of the feet accommodated to the subject'.[1] A manuscript account of action agrees: 'And to stamp with the foot in great contentions is not unseemly.'[2] If we are to rely on the stage direction, the actor playing Ragan did this in *The True Chronicle History of King Leir and His Three Daughters*: 'She reads the letter, frowns and stamps'. And the Messenger describes:

> See how she knits her brow, and bites her lips,
> And stamps, and makes a dumb-show of disdain,
> Mix'd with revenge and violent extremes.[3]

Mr. Spenser found himself stamping his foot because of the frustration he experienced as Aumerle, equally involved in 'revenge and violent extremes'. This nobleman, cousin to both the new and the deposed king, has just been challenged and accused of treason by a man of much lower rank. To meet one of so low a rank is beneath the dignity of a nobleman of the standing of Aumerle; it is tantamount to a loss of honour. But to let the accusation pass uncontested is equally to submit to dishonour (IV. i. 19–25). When this actor fully realized the intolerable conflict of 'extremes' raging within him, he inevitably stamped his foot in frustration as well as rage as he flung down his gage to wipe out the insult. This was an example of emotion expressing itself naturally in action in the way in which Thomas Wright envisaged it with his analogy of the wind passing through the trumpet.

What is the relevance of these details of the way in which 'renaissance gestures' have been used successfully by modern actors? This success in no way proves that Elizabethan actors must also have used them. It does establish beyond any doubt, however, the fact that this acting described by Bulwer and fellow writers is not a stereotyped, conventional or formal art. It is one

---

[1] See T. W. Baldwin, *William Shakespeare's Small Latine & Lesse Greeke* (1944), i. 328.
[2] MS. Ashmole 768, p. 541.
[3] Ed. W. W. Greg and R. W. Bond (1907), sigs. E1r–E1v.

which struck modern actors, audiences, and critics, all highly suspicious of it, as in fact a natural outcome of the thought, emotion, and desire within a performer who imagined what it would be like to be the character he was playing, and who forced his soul to his own conceit. Actors not trained to express themselves as a sort of second nature in this art soon found how it helped them to realize an inner experience as an integration of intellectual, emotional, and physical activity. The fact that they could do this in this century suggests that it was possible for actors to do the same in Shakespeare's day, when there existed a living tradition to which a boy was introduced in practice from his earliest days at school.

It is in Elizabethan sources that we find the evidence which proves how relevant was the 'external action' of the 'orator' to that of the player. As we saw in Chapter One, everything contributes to support Wright's statement that 'in the substance of external action for most part orators and stage-players agree'. And often when we learn what was taught to the orator it proves to be what Stanislavski calls 'real action' and not a merely external flowing line. Bulwer's examples of the way in which 'the present state of the will' is communicated in gesture are often taken from what he actually saw in the day-to-day life of seventeenth-century England. Some of these have already been treated (pp. 14–20). Another looks innocuous enough as used by the figure labelled Cicero on the engraved title of *Chironomia* (Fig. 1). It once achieved the notoriety, however, of being denounced in Bacon's report on duelling to the Star Chamber. Bulwer calls it *Ironiam infligo* (Q, Fig. 4) and says: 'To bend the middle finger while it stiffly resteth upon the thumb, and so in jesting-wise to let it off, is a trivial expression whereby we with a fillip inflict a trifling punishment.' In the first half of the seventeenth century it was accepted that 'this slighting expression of the fingers gives such a slur of disgrace if used to men that it hath been thought such a disparagement as wounded a tender reputation'. Bulwer is talking of contemporary life, not of something that we can disregard as an alleged element of 'stereotype delivery'. Francis Bacon, 'being then His Majesty's Attorney-General, informs against the hot-spirited gallants of those times, who pretended a defect in our law that it hath provided no remedy for fillips'. Bulwer himself regretted that such trivial things, simply because 'they have got upon them the stamp of a disgrace', should be regarded as 'a mortal wound to the reputation'.[1] If this 'fillip' led to duels in real life, it is hardly too fanciful to assume it may well have been used on the stage. It certainly was used by 'orators' when inflicting an irony upon opponents in a speech.

We cannot be sure that a gesture called *Chirothripsia* was in common usage in Bulwer's day, although he mentions it as having been used by Henry VIII on his death-bed as a speechless sign of his sincere wish to be reconciled penitently to Heaven. *Chirothripsia* ('to press hard and wring another's hand') is to hold the other person's hand between one's palms, interlacing the fingers round it. 'This gesture,' says Bulwer, 'as it is a token of duty and reverential love, Coriolanus used towards his mother, Volumnia, when, overcome by her earnest persuasions to withdraw his army from Rome, he cried out, "Oh, Mother! What have you done to me?"' At this moment he is described as 'holding her hard by the right hand'.[2] Plutarch is given as the source. In fact, however, he does not actually say that Coriolanus wrung his mother's hand in this manner as a 'token of duty and reverential love', but he describes the incident almost exactly as it is given by Bulwer.

And with these words, herself, his wife and children, fell down upon their knees before him. Martius, seeing that, could refrain no longer, but went straight and lifted her up, crying out, 'Oh, Mother, what have you done to me?' And holding her hard by the right hand, 'Oh, Mother,' said he, 'You have won a happy victory for your country.'[3]

Although North's Plutarch has long been recognized as a

[1] *Chirol.*, pp. 177 f.   [2] *Chirol.*, pp. 116 ff.
[3] *The Life of Caius Martius Coriolanus*, tr. North (1579), repr. W. J. Craig and R. H. Case, *The Tragedy of Coriolanus* (1922), p. lx.

source for Shakespeare's Coriolanus, it has been common of recent years to overlook the similarity between North's 'And holding her hard by the right hand' and the stage direction in the First Folio, *Holds her by the hand silent*. Of course, it is by no means certain that the first actor of Shakespeare's Coriolanus wrung Volumnia's hand on the stage in the manner which Bulwer describes. But Poussin painted Coriolanus doing it; and this is how he holds his mother's hand in Hayman's illustration (based on Poussin) to Hanmer's edition of Shakespeare (1746).

Many of the gestures which Bulwer treats in *Chironomia* were obviously designed primarily to be used in formal oratory. Such are the two described as Canons IV and VI:

The gentle and well-ordered hand thrown forth by a moderate projection, the fingers unfolding themselves in the motion, and the shoulders a little slackened, affords a familiar force to any plain continued speech or uniform discourse; and much graceth any matter that requires to be handled with a more lofty style, which we would fain fully present in a more gorgeous excess of words.

The comeliness of this action (which best suits with them who remove and shift their standing) appears herein, that by this emanation of the arm and delivery of gesture, speech is so well pronounced and poured forth, that it seems to flow out of the hand.

But the second gesture is quite different in effect:

The hand restrained and kept in is an argument of modesty and frugal pronunciation, a still and quiet action, suitable to a mild and remiss declamation.

Another gesture of this sort is:

The hand collected, the fingers looking downwards, then turned and resolved, is a set form accommodated to their intention who would openly produce their reasons.

The artificial conceit of this action is, that it seems as it were indeed to bring forth with it some hidden matter to make the argument in hand more rhetorically apparent.[1]

---

[1] *Chiron.*, pp. 30 f., 32; Canon VIII, p. 35.

Although these and others like them belong to formal oratory, they could still be used whenever a character in a play is pleading or arguing formally; as when Ulysses, the Archbishop of Canterbury, Antony, and Brutus make their formal speeches in Shakespeare's plays. But the gestures need not have been restricted to such occasions. I have found that they can be used by modern actors quite validly to communicate emotion and purpose at any moment, both in monologue and dialogue, or even in dumb-show, as with the performance of the Ghost in *Hamlet* which has already been mentioned (pp. 49 f.). The use of the two hands for an antithesis by Horatio in this production has also been described. This gesture was even more expressive of the thought and emotion in an amateur performance in the University of Bristol of Juliet's:

> My husband lives that Tybalt would have slain,
> And Tybalt's dead that would have slain my husband.

And having experienced the effect of the following 'action' when used to communicate emotion and purpose by modern actors, I have no difficulty in believing it was at least as expressive as an element in the acting of the Elizabethans:

We may use likewise the advantage of both hands when we would present by some ample gesture the immensity of things; some space's far and wide extent, a great number, almost infinite, large affections, or when the voice is re-iterate by conduplication.[1]

Conduplication is defined by Puttenham as 'a manner of repetition, when one and the self word doth begin and end many verses in suit'. He gives this example:

> Who made me shent for her love's sake?
> Mine own mistress.
> Who would not seem my part to take?
> Mine own mistress.
> What made me first so well content?
> Her courtesy.
> What makes me now so sore repent?
> Her cruelty.[2]

---

[1] *Chiron.*, pp. 58 f.   [2] Op. cit., pp. 199–200.

The figure is used in Antony's speech on Caesar. The gesture which Bulwer describes enables the speaker's irony to be far more expressive in its repetitions, 'For Brutus is an honourable man', 'But Brutus says he was ambitious', 'And Brutus is an honourable man'.

It is difficult to know how far to be guided by Bulwer's account of the significance of gestures with the left hand alone. He not only repeats the customary warning of the classical rhetoricians against this practice, but offers some pages of quotation respecting its connexion with the notion of dishonesty. That this may have some relevance to renaissance social custom is suggested by the fact that, as he notes, theft was punished in his day by a brand on the left thumb for a first offence. He surmises that the practice originally involved some symbolism relating to the tradition that associates the left hand with theft:

And if it be lawful to divine of the legality of this law-check, I should think that there lies some concealed symbol in the device, and that the estates assembled had regard to the felonious pro-cacity and craft of this guileful hand, which is prone by a sly insinuation with more subtle secrecy to present itself to any sinister intention, and doth no sooner move to such actions, but every finger proves a lime-twig.[1]

Gesture LXIII in *Chirologia* is called *Furacitatem noto* (Marked Y in Fig. 3): 'To put forth the left hand as it were by stealth is their significant endeavour who have an intent un-seen to purloin and convey away some thing.' It is from this, says Bulwer, that the adage is derived, '*Utitur manu sinistra*, which, translated, in the proverbial sense is took up against cheats and pilfering fellows, who by a thievish sleight of hand, and sly way of robbery, can bereave one of a thing unperceived.'

There is much evidence to show that this was the meaning of the left hand for antiquity, when it had 'the noted property . . . to be covered, and to keep as it were a recluse in the bosom, or to be carried wrapped up in a cloak, lurking closely and lying as

---

[1] *Chirol.*, p. 134.

it were in ambuscado to entrap'. He seems to be talking of his own times as well, however; especially in the passage declaring that the left hand 'being commonly hid and involved in the bosom of a gown or cloak . . . that doing nothing and devoted to rest, yet being at liberty and ready to handle, it will be doing, and somewhat of other men's suffers for it'.[1]

The miniature illustrations to early medieval manuscripts of Terence show the left hand always wrapped in the toga, or holding the scarf which hangs round the neck of a worker, or a tool or implement, except for a few occasions when the speaker is involved in deceiving another person of the drama.[2] Here we may have the origin of the habit of nineteenth-century tragedians of keeping the left hand for the most part in the bosom. Phelps's addiction to it led to his being described irreverently as looking as if he were perpetually searching for a flea. Certainly there was some sort of prohibition against the use of the left hand alone on the eighteenth-century stage, but it is not clear how strictly or consistently this was observed in practice.

It seems quite possible that, whatever may have been the social significance of using the left hand, it was associated with a stigma, if not merely the stigma of stealing, in the acting of the Elizabethan theatre. This possibility is strengthened by what is said in an incident in Chapman's *An Humorous Day's Mirth* (1599).[3] Lemot enters wounded 'with his arm in a scarf', and is urged to answer the Queen's question, 'how fares the King?' He starts with an apology for the impoliteness of using his left hand:

> Bear with my rudeness, then, in telling it,
> For, alas, you see I can but act it with my left hand!
> This is my gesture now.   (Sc. XIII. 14–16.)

This passage suggests, first, that his account would normally have involved 'acting it' with the right hand; and, second, that it was discourteous to 'act it' with the left.

---

[1] *Chirol.*, pp. 133 ff.
[2] L. W. Jones and C. R. Morey, *The Miniatures of the Manuscripts of Terence prior to the Thirteenth century*. The Plates (n.d.).
[3] Ed. Parrott (1913), p. 87.

Certainly Lemot on the Elizabethan stage at this moment was in agreement with the tradition according to which Bulwer's *Cautio* XXVI in *Chironomia* declares: 'The left hand of itself alone is most incompetent to the performance of any perfect action: yet sometimes it doth, but very rarely.'[1] He gives two of these rare exceptions:

The left hand thrust forth with the palm turned backward, the left shoulder raised, so that it may aptly consent with the head bearing to the right hand, agrees with their intention who refuse, abhor, detest, or abominate some execrable thing, against which their minds are bent as a distasteful object, which they would seem to chase away and repel.

and:

The left hand explained into a palm obtains a form of perspicuity.[2]

There are more pages of discussion of the solecism of using the left hand in Section 25 of Bulwer's Apocrypha of Action in *Chironomia*. Section 26 observes that a priest ought not to bless or dismiss his auditors with the left hand by itself. 'For an ecclesiastical orator to bless or dismiss his auditors with the left hand is a solecism in manual divinity.'[3]

It is difficult for the modern English mind to associate with Elizabethan acting a tradition such as this warning not to use the left hand. If we are justified in fact in assuming that it was the practice of Elizabethan actors not to use the left hand alone, except in specific cases involving theft or deceit, this does not mean that we are to think that their art was formal or stereotyped. For the Elizabethans may merely have been presenting on the stage what was true of social behaviour off it, just as today our normal social custom of shaking hands with the right, not the left, hand is followed by actors on the stage, without their art becoming formal, rather than natural.

---

[1] p. 142.
[2] Canon XXXII, pp. 52 f.; Canon XXXIII, p. 53.
[3] pp. 123 ff.

If we were to apply this tradition to stage-playing it would provide a reasonable meaning to Hamlet's cryptic reference to 'these pickers and stealers'. They would be the fingers and thumb of the left hand, which the Prince raises as to swear an oath: as this is on the left hand it expresses ironically the insistence that Rosencrantz is mistaken in his assurance that Hamlet 'once did love' him.

And if the tradition that every finger of the left hand is a lime-twig extended to the stage, then it was this hand which the actor of Autolycus described as 'the snapper up of unconsidered trifles'. Autolycus boasts that he was 'littered under Mercury'; and 'Mercurialists' is the term used by Bulwer of those 'who address themselves to filch'. He also quotes Martial as an authority for the assertion that the classical Autolycus was expert 'in the sly feats of this hand':

Non erat Autolici tam piceata manus.[1]

Renaissance accounts of 'external action' tell us less about voice than about face, hand, and movement, probably because it is impossible to describe accurately the sound of a voice expressing emotion and purpose. Again we are concerned with what it was normal to do rather than with a rigid convention of what must be done. There is a certain amount of evidence to show that at school the teachers aimed at encouraging clear articulation with well-disciplined flexibility, and a good range of tone, volume, and intensity. With the first days at school began a systematic drill which would equip a boy mentally and vocally to fulfil all the demands that the speaking and acting of verse and prose would make on him.

Clear enunciation was essential. 'From the first entrance', says Brinsley, boys should be taught 'to pronounce everything audibly, leisurely, distinctly and naturally; sounding out specially the last syllable that each word may be fully understood.'[2] He stresses the importance of the last syllable, not so that it should become exaggerated, but to overcome the natural tendency of

[1] *Chirch.*, pp. 134, 136.   [2] Op. cit., p. 212.

the untrained reader to swallow it. At Ipswich the first form, whose boys were learning 'only the eight parts of speech', was nevertheless to be started correctly in the best habits of reading and speaking. 'Let your principal attention be to form their tender articulation, so as in a full, elegant tone of voice they may pronounce the elements they are taught; for it is possible to mould their rude materials into any form'. So Wolsey instructed his masters at his refounding of the school. In the fourth form the same care was to be observed, only now with 'Virgil, the Prince of Poets'. The boys were to be made to pronounce 'his majestic lines in a deep, full articulation'.[1] Bury St. Edmunds is typical of the English grammar school of the time, where the masters were told to 'take diligent heed and beware for their scholars' distinct and plain pronunciation'.[2]

But monotony was to be avoided. The boys are not to speak 'as a boy who is saying his lesson', says Brinsley.[3] At Bury St. Edmunds, boys who were being taught 'the first elements of grammar' were to be carefully prevented from uttering words 'at random and without understanding like parrots, but are to pronounce with pleasing and apt modulation tempered with variety'. When able to read and speak Latin they must still not utter words 'without full and perfect understanding of the matter and meaning thereof'. The master had to make sure 'that they read not nor speak in one time, but that diligent heed be given to the due accent in pronunciation'.[4]

The few facts which are known about voice training suggest that this employed methods still known today. Vives says that it is the task of the singing teacher. Zouche's play, *The Sophister* (1639), has an incident in which one character rehearses another in 'pronouncing', using fingers to gag him, a method still used by teachers of voice production today.[5] What is said by Quintilian on this subject is echoed by renaissance writers. Thomas Wilson recommends 'exercise of the body, fasting, moderation

[1] Baldwin, op. cit., i. 123 f., 152.   [2] Ibid., i. 301, 306.
[3] Op. cit., p. 178.   [4] See Baldwin, i. 306.
[5] Act IV, Sc. iii, sig. G4ᵛ.

in meat and drink, gaping wide, or singing plain-song, and counterfeiting those that do speak distinctly'. He laments that musicians no longer 'put gags in children's mouths, that they might pronounce distinctly'.[1] He was obviously mistaken, unless the practice had been newly revived in Zouche's time. Fraunce has the usual suggestions for developing the voice and keeping it in trim:

The practice and exercise is all in all: learn therefore some such speech wherein are contained all or most varieties of voice, and oftentimes use to pronounce the same in such order and with as great heed as if thou were to utter it in some great assembly. Walking a little after supper, anointing, moderation of diet, and such-like bodily pleasures keep the voice in temper.[2]

In his educational treatise, *Positions* (1581), Mulcaster, the famous headmaster of Merchant Taylors' School, praises an exercise 'both the first in rank, and the best mean to make good pronouncing of anything, in any auditory, and therefore an exercise not impertinent to scholars'. It consisted of making children who could read recite aloud 'either iambic verses, or elegies, or other such numbers, which with their current carry the memory on', this being done as loudly as possible and with due attention to meaning and variety. Children who had not yet learned to read said 'such things as they could remember, which were to be spoken aloud, and admitted any change of voice in the uttering, now harsh and hard, now smooth and sweet.'[3] The exercise was variously known as *vociferatio*, loudspeaking and crying-out.

These facts, taken into account with the demands made upon a speaker by Elizabethan dramatic verse, support the conjecture that actors were trained to produce a sustained tone, based upon diaphragm support, for centuries a practice normal to singers and actors, and still employed today. For the structure and meaning of Elizabethan verse demands from a speaker breath and flexibility of tone which cannot otherwise be forthcoming. The

[1] *The Art of Rhetoric* (1560), ed. Mair (1909), p. 219.
[2] Op. cit., p. 120.   [3] pp. 55-58.

demands on the actor are even greater. He has to move about the stage and to maintain a sustained emotional pressure: he cannot succeed without the reserve of air in the lungs provided by this support. The method relies upon diaphragm pressure for increased volume, while at the same time integration of thought, emotion, and larynx provides tone of the required pitch, length, and intensity. There is no reason why this method of voice training and production should not have been used in Shakespeare's day. Elizabethan actors may not have used exactly the same methods as are described by Garcia, and in our own day by Franklyn Kelsey and Julian Gardiner, but it is reasonable to suppose that the differences were not great.

Hamlet's warning not to chant and whine, elongating syllables too much, is directed against one of the defects which easily develops when this method of voice production is misused: 'but if you mouth it, as many of our players do, I had as lief the town-crier spoke my lines'. The town-crier both mouths and chants, chiefly because he does not speak his words with meaning. In fact it seems that the different kinds of bad speaking were the results in Shakespeare's day, as in our own, of not being conscious of the meaning of every word in relation to all the others, and of not communicating that meaning according to the word's 'intention'. Not only a chant, but monotony is produced in this way. The speech comes 'trippingly' when the mind and emotions behind the larynx, jaw, lips, and tongue are responding accurately to the words in a particular, not a general, way, and when the will is involved actively. Then the changes in pitch come trippingly, thanks to the author's verbal structure which is being embodied in sound, and thanks also to the fact that, as Bulwer reminds us, 'Nature assigns each motion of the mind', not only its proper gesture and countenance, but its tone.

I have already explained elsewhere that the well-controlled sustained tone was probably the essential foundation of what was known as 'cadenced speech' after the Restoration.[1] It gives a speaking which is more musical than that of ordinary conver-

[1] See *The Tragic Actor*, pp. 15, 28–32, 394 f.

sation; the music derives from the fact that tone is produced and articulated precisely, attaining a variety, and communicating a complexity of meaning as the direct result of the author's art as well as the actor's. The tones are natural to the meaning, and the resultant articulate sound is also what the meaning naturally requires, no syllable too long, no consonant slurred, no frequencies of pitch that do not belong to the normal speaking range. But when the actor was in any way incompetent, either in his inner realization or his external technique of expression, then defects developed, as chanting, monotony or rant. This last is, and no doubt was, the result not only of insincerely realized emotion, but also of incompetently produced tone (possibly itself due to the insincerity of the emotion). This is what Hamlet begs the player to avoid when his specially written speech is performed.

The mention by the Chorus in the Prologue of *Romeo and Juliet* of 'the two hours' traffic of our stage' has often led to discussion as to the speed of Elizabethan speaking. In my experience modern actors, whose speech and action operate in accordance with the principles treated in this chapter and in Chapter Two, are able to speak their lines swiftly without gabbling. Their attention to the structure of the lines, and to every word in that structure as an expression of the character's inner life, enables them to communicate more effectively when speaking swiftly than is usually the case with actors speaking more slowly today. I do not know how long the average performance took in Elizabethan England; no doubt it varied with the length of the play and the place in which it was played. But I can easily believe that Shakespeare's company acted *Romeo and Juliet* in two hours, or very little more. I have directed amateurs in an uncut version of the play on an 'Elizabethan-type' stage, and they rarely exceeded two hours and ten minutes and never took longer than two hours and a quarter. Their acting, of course, was not good; but their speaking was clear and could not only be understood, but communicated to the audience an experience of the imagery. It seems to me that Elizabethan actors were able to perform more swiftly than modern actors and to communicate much more completely, not only because their audience was more accustomed to listening, but because of their own training and abilities as actors.

It was to train them away from such vocal defects as chant, monotony and rant that the Elizabethan schoolmaster concentrated on teaching the boys to speak with an 'apt modulation'.[1] At Winchester, Christopher Johnson congratulated his pupils that they had not only shown their command of delivery but were able now to teach others, both bodily movement and 'in the voice a certain amount of elevation, depression and modulation'.[2] When modulation was 'apt', the voice changed in pitch, resonance, intensity, and volume as a result of communicating not merely the sense of every word, but the emotion and the intention expressed precisely in it. The resulting sounds and the variations of pace were due to and expressive of intellectual and emotional co-ordination.

It is clear that the Elizabethan actor was trained physically and intellectually as well as psychologically to respond precisely to the precision of a dramatist's writing. Voice, face, and body were able to communicate exactly what was being realized no less exactly within. This means that the swift changes of emotion expressed in a dramatic text were communicated in a poetry of sound, movement, and facial expression: what were known as 'transitions' in the eighteenth and nineteenth centuries were probably known to the Elizabethan stage as well. Certainly the training made such things possible and Elizabethan texts often demand them.

[1] See charter of Bury St. Edmunds, quoted on p. 67, *supra*.
[2] Baldwin, op. cit., i. 328.

CHAPTER FOUR

The Greatest Pleasure of a Play

THE Elizabethan actor was a man or boy who was able to seem to his audience to be the very person, man or woman, whom he represented in the performance of a play. His tones of voice were those in which it was natural to communicate the meaning expressed by the author in the words which were being articulated: the emphasis, in its details of pitch, length, and stress, was what the 'very person' would use to express himself in real life if using these words. The fact that these actual words might not be used did not matter to the actor behaving as if they were: he spoke both realistic and unrealistic lines as they ought to be spoken to evoke a response from an audience to an acknowledged performance of each individual work of art. His speaking suited both character and style, since style and meaning are inseparable.

The actor's appearance and movement served the same two purposes simultaneously. Face, eyes, gesture, movement, attitude, communicated naturally what is within the imaginary character, with adjustments of such matters as pace and rhythm to the style of the lines as well as to the individual character-image. 'Voice' and 'action' together enabled the actor to be a creative instrument ideally suited to the needs of Elizabethan plays and audiences.

The Elizabethan play, like any other, is an imagining of persons involved in a shaped plot, inter-acting with one another in incidents which have implications for them and for their audiences and their author. The mixture of realistic and unrealistic elements in the medium as the Elizabethan author used it allows him, while imagining an incident or nexus of incidents, to express more implications than is usually possible in a play which is consistently realistic. The implications, the literary quality of the lines, the shaping of the plot, are and were apparent to the reader. Thanks to the actor, these aspects of a play could be communicated to the Elizabethan audience at least as powerfully and completely as they are perceived by the reader with the words on the page in front of him.

It is very rare for an Elizabethan play to have this effect in performance today. To some extent this is due to the laziness of the modern ear, even to a degree of actual deafness as a result of the noise of modern living, and of course to the fact that the modern mind and ear are not alert to specific details of Elizabethan literary texts, even when these are to be seen on the printed page. Nevertheless, despite the fact that an Elizabethan audience was in every way more capable of responding to individual elements of articulate sound, both as sound and meaning, the comparative dullness of the modern response in the theatre is due even more to changes which have taken place in acting; and these are themselves the result of changes over a long period both in drama and theatrical practice. My experience in teaching acting students to act Shakespeare, in coaching professional actors and directing professional casts has shown me that it is possible to induce a more powerful and detailed response from audiences whose minds are not attuned to the precise recognition and appreciation of individual elements of a dramatist's style. There is good reason to believe that one of the greatest, if not the greatest, of pleasures of performance for Elizabethans lay in the ability of their actors to seem to be the actual men and women to an audience whose experience of a play as a work of literature was strengthened, rather than weakened, by this fact.

For that Elizabethan playgoer, Sir Richard Baker, who saw Burbage and Alleyn perform, the greatest pleasure of a play lay in the acting, 'in the gracefulness of the action'. This had to be 'fitted to the speech', however; and the speech itself pleased him with what he calls its 'ingeniousness' when it in its turn was 'fitted to the person'. From the author's conception of his character and its needs comes the speech which has also to be well written as literature in its own right; the acting then does justice to each of these elements simultaneously:

> For it is not the scurrility and ribaldry that gives the content-ment . . . but it is the ingeniousness of the speech, when it is fitted to the person; and the gracefulness of the action, when it is fitted to the speech; and therefore a play read hath not half the pleasure of a play acted: for though it have the pleasure of ingenious speeches, yet it wants the pleasure of graceful action: and we may well acknowledge that gracefulness of action is the greatest pleasure of a play; seeing it is the greatest pleasure of (the art of pleasure) rhetoric.[1]

What Baker calls 'gracefulness of action' is the result of an identified actor representing the character 'to the life'. When this happened, voice, face, and gesture communicated the meaning of the words for the character as thought, emotion, and desire, as if the actor were the person he represented. He was able to do this, moreover, only because he understood the relation of the individual words to one another, both as expressive of what is within the character and as a verbal structure in their own right. In these circumstances, to articulate the words was to do all that was required for 'the person' and for 'the ingeniousness of the speech' to whom it was fitted.

If we are to believe Baker, his was a normal response to a normal performance. He is describing an aesthetic experience in which are fused an imagining of characters and incidents, a responding as if the actor were the man represented, and an awareness that he was an actor giving a competent, good, or superb performance.

There is a modern habit of referring to these elements in the Elizabethan response to an unrealistic play as if they were peculiarly Elizabethan. But I have known modern audiences respond to the performance of Elizabethan drama in essentially the same way. At the Mermaid Theatre in St. John's Wood in 1951 and in the Studio Theatre in the University of Bristol some

---

[1] Op. cit., pp. 34 f.

months later, performances of the first scene of *Hamlet* under my direction evoked from members of the audience the amazed avowal that they had not thought it possible to look at a modern man playing the part of the Ghost on a brightly lit stage, and, while knowing that it was a modern actor, react as if it were indeed the Ghost imagined by the Elizabethan writer. There is nothing specifically Elizabethan in such a response: for centuries theatrical audiences have been aware of the skill of playwright and actor, even as they accept the actor as if he were the character come to life. This still happens except to the most naïve members of an audience. And even in the heyday of naturalism, whatever naturalist theory might have to say about consistent illusion, conscious admiration for the consistency of the realism in acting and staging was one element in the audience's response. There is no essential difference in this response from that of the Elizabethans. What is different is the quality of the 'ingeniousness' of the speech fitted to the person, and consequently of the virtuosity of the actor playing him. But it is probable that the Elizabethan audience had a greater variety of elements in the performance to enjoy: there was the author's skill in writing, the actor's in imitating, in delivering 'ingenious' speeches, everything combining as a response to the whole quality of a work of art in its performance. Baker derived much pleasure from reading a play; but he found it less enjoyable than a play acted. The reader is restricted to the words and their meaning; but performance gave the actor's voice, countenance, and body. The play read had 'the pleasure of ingenious speeches', but it lacked 'the pleasure of graceful action'.

Baker is saying nothing about the essential difference between a play read and acted: he is talking about the difference in the pleasure which each gives. He actually suggests that in essence he made no distinction between the read and the acted play as such, asking: 'And what doth a player else, but only say without book that which we may read without book?'[1] This should not be confused with the inadequate notions of those modern critics

[1] Ibid., p. 43.

who insist despairingly that what they call vaguely, if passionately, 'the poetry' of a play is only to be apprehended by a reader, that performance is too gross an instrument for so subtle a work of art. Whatever Baker may have thought about the relation of a play read to a play acted, he knew from experience that there was more pleasure in the play performed.

There seems no reason to doubt that other Elizabethans shared Baker's view. Heywood describes the Englishman responding to performance 'as being wrapt in contemplation', a perfect analogy for the concentrated imagining of a play by a spectator watching and listening to actors acting. Here, again, it was 'as if the personator were the man personated', yet at the same time performance entailed speaking well, which meant 'with judgment to observe his comma's, colons and full points, his parentheses, his breathing spaces and distinctions'.[1] We may ask, nevertheless, how many members of an average audience, and how many audiences as a whole at a house like The Red Bull, appreciated the relationship of the acting to the ingeniousness of the speeches and the persons to whom these were fitted. Dekker suggests in a Prologue that a good dramatist could give his players lines which would affect even the least educated members of the audience in theatres of this sort. Having deplored the degradation of popular drama by popular taste, he asks for the playwright who can hold this audience with better things:

> Give me that man,
> Who when the plague of an impostum'd brain's
> Breaking out infects a theatre, and hotly reigns,
> Killing the hearers' hearts, that the vast rooms
> Stand empty, like so many dead men's tombs,
> Can call the banish'd auditor home, and tie
> His ear with golden chains to his melody,
> Can draw with adamantine pen, even creatures
> Forg'd out of th' hammer, on tip-toe to reach up,
> And, from rare silence, clap their brawny hands,
> T'applaud what their charm'd soul scarce understands.

[1] Op. cit., sigs. B4ʳ, C4ʳ.

That man give me, whose breast fill'd by the Muses
With raptures, into a second them infuses,
Can give an actor sorrow, rage, joy, passion,
Whilst he again, by self-same agitation,
Commands the hearers, sometimes drawing out tears,
Then smiles, and fills them both with hopes and fears.
That man give me. And to be such a one
Our poet this day strives, or to be none.[1]

In another Prologue, Dekker writes as if audiences were critical
of a play's qualities as literature during the actual performance,
even of a new play:

A play, expected long, makes the audience look
For wonders:—that each scene should be a book,
Compos'd to all perfection; each one comes
And brings a play in's head with him: up he sums
What he would of a Roaring Girl have writ;
If that he finds not here, he mews at it.[2]

It seems that, thanks to the actor, the Elizabethan spectator
in the theatre missed nothing that he could derive from a play
as a reader with a true respect for the author's intention as that
is communicated in his words. It seems, too, that the spectator's
response was richer than that of the reader in that it involved
an experience of the actor's disciplined skill and creative acting
in the service of the author. For the moment, however, we are
concerned not with 'the pleasure of graceful action' which the
reader missed, but with the poetic wealth which was no less
accessible to the spectator. The reader derived from the text an
experience in which he was conscious of such things as the
author's skill with individual words, of the text's verbal music,
of the quality of the images, in each case as literature and as an
expression of the inner life of the character. From his understanding of the inner life of the characters and their relation to
one another he perceived the shaping of imagined incidents in

---

[1] *If this be not a Good Play, the Devil is in It* (1612), ed. F. T. Bowers, *The Dramatic Works of Thomas Dekker*, iii (1958), 121 f.
[2] *The Roaring Girl* (1611), ed. Bowers, op. cit., p. 12.

a plot; and as his knowledge of the whole play grew with his reading, there came an awareness of the implications involved in the action for its author. All this could be accessible to the spectator when the actors had mastered the play as a whole; he could respond to their individual speeches in the same way, noticing how the action progressed, and its implications.

I have found that when modern actors make use of Elizabethan methods of preparation and have an attitude to the play corresponding to what seems to have been the Elizabethan one, it is possible for them to communicate to an audience the meaning of a word, image or incident, not only for the characters they are representing, but for the author who is conscious of theme or irony, and who has not imagined his characters as having any inkling of such knowledge. For instance, Shakespeare has imagined Lear consistently as a person incapable of mastering his resentment at his treatment by Goneril and Regan, as a man who must threaten them with revenge, not because he has the slightest hope of ever being in a position again to punish them, but because he wants so much to be able to one day. The actor who creates this Lear at this moment contributes to the audiences' perception of an irony which the character never knows. For unknown to the King, there is in fact a plot to reinstate him; and when the two daughters, Cornwall, and Edmund learn of its existence they determine to destroy him before he can destroy them. The tragic irony is deepened even more by the fact that when he is taken prisoner, the actor playing Lear will have created for the audience a man interested in nothing more than living what is left of his life as a grateful and contented object of Cordelia's love: and for that it is enough for them to share imprisonment.

To communicate to the audience the irony of which the character is not aware, all that the actor has to do, even today, is create the character as a result of understanding and making use of the relation of each word in his role to every other as he speaks them, both as literature and as an expression of that character's inner life. If this is so today, it seems reasonable to suggest that the task could be accomplished at least as well in Shakespeare's day. In each case, success presupposes competent acting, of course.

It seems that the competent Elizabethan actor using the images for the purposes of the character could make his audience respond to them at least as powerfully as when reading the play themselves. Florizel's delight in Perdita's dancing is such that he could wish her to do nothing but dance, for her whole existence to be one of movement, just as a wave of the sea has its whole existence in movement: when the water is still, there is no wave. Whatever else there may be for him in the words, he is primarily expressing his love for the kind of person that Perdita is to him, for an essential quality of her which reveals itself in her dancing: and the image of the wave, always in motion so long as it is a wave, expresses the intensity of his love for the quality which is embodied so perfectly in her movement, and which he wants her always to retain.

> When you do dance, I wish you
> A wave o' th' sea, that you might ever do
> Nothing but that; move still, still so,
> And own no other function.
>
> (*The Winter's Tale*, IV. iv. 140–3.)

When an actor had related each word in this passage to the thought, emotion, and desire of Florizel, the character, he could use the image to communicate his wish to obtain his objective. His own imaging of the wave was probably more than visual; he responded as to something heard, touched, and even tasted with a trace of salt sea-air or spray on lips, tongue, and palate. This did not evoke equivalent physiological responses in the audience, but it let him evoke in them at least as powerful a mental picture and its meaning as they could derive from their own reading. Moreover, they would realize that Florizel is not longing for Perdita to move for ever, but to retain for ever the quality which is so admirable in her.

Today an actor creates his role out of his concentration upon every word of his text, imagined in terms of thought, emotion, and desire in the given circumstances of the action. I see no reason to suppose that the Elizabethans did not do the same: indeed, the evidence considered earlier reveals that they were determined to allow every word 'to have his intention according to his signification'. Then, as now, the quality of the writing was of fundamental importance. Today, when the actor has a script in which precisely used words express all that is relevant, fully developed by the author, then these words themselves are found to exercise powerful control over the playing of the part. This does not mean that the actor is put in a straight-jacket. His performance is none the less a genuinely creative imagining; but in their individual precision, the words call on him to make use of them for equally precise and specific purposes. They indicate to him the goal for which he must strive, while leaving him free as a creative artist to attain it by means of them in his individual way. It seems that this was true of Elizabethan acting as well. In certain circumstances, moreover, the control or guidance of the Elizabethan words is more detailed than that of a modern script. But however precisely they might guide him and indicate his task, the Elizabethan actor was still free to fulfil his individuality as an artist.

When he acted a speech containing figures of words the actor was guided by a comparatively intricate structure in which relationships between individual words revealed to him what had to be communicated for the character he was playing. In his communication he made use of these relationships between words to represent the character as if he were the very man, and they were apparent in his voice as articulate sound. The 'ingeniousness' of his lines and 'the person' to whom they were fitted, were for him and his audience one and the same. The more completely he was identified, the more natural were his tones, emphasis, appearance, and the more completely did he convey to the spectators both the inner life of the character and the ingeniousness of the author's speeches. Flamineo's sneer, his determination to persist, his resentment at his lot and at his mother for not having provided for him and for objecting to his own efforts at making an improvement, are valid at this moment in the action: the author's ingeniousness shows itself in the economy with which all this is expressed in the play of words:

what means have you
To keep me from the galley or the gallows?
(*The White Devil*, I. ii.)[1]

In the same way 'ingeniousness of the speeches' and the character of the 'person' are fused in Macbeth's

If th' assassination
Could trammel up the consequence, and catch
With his surcease, success.

In a passage such as Rosalind's account of the meeting of Celia and Oliver with their falling in love at first sight, every actor was guided both by sense and structure in speaking, so that what the eye of the reader sees was perceived both by ear and eye of spectator. In this particular case, the words in italics were heard in their relationship to one another by the audience:

For your brother and my sister no sooner *met* but they *look'd*; no sooner *look'd* but they *lov'd*; no sooner *lov'd* but they *sigh'd*; no sooner *sigh'd* but they ask'd one another *the reason*; no sooner knew *the reason* but they sought the *remedy*.
(*As You Like It*, v. ii. 30–34.)

Whoever spoke these lines failed to communicate all their meaning if he did not make the figure 'manifest' in his speaking; and conversely an identified actor who made them manifest could not fail to communicate their meaning.[2] This holds good of modern acting, too.

It is in such details that competent and incompetent performances showed themselves immediately. Here are 'rules' to which actors must adhere. They are rules, however, which insist on each word being used for the purpose for which the author has selected it; and that purpose includes the creation of the character by an

[1] Ed. J. A. Symonds (1948), p. 19.   [2] See pp. 25–40 above.

identified actor as well as making manifest the ingeniousness of the speeches. Structure, thought, emotion, and desire are all indicated precisely for the actor; but he is left independent as a creative artist to communicate them. He had often no choice when it came to the words to be emphasized, but he was free to choose any tone, any pace which allowed him as an individual best to emphasize them.

Every actor of this passage would create a pattern of sound which would make manifest the same figures, the same relationship of words as meaning and as pattern. But the actual sounds used by each actor, it seems to me, must have been determined by his personal characteristics, his voice, his mind, his feeling of emotion. His use of actual sounds, the pace and rhythm of his speaking, derived from his full use of the words in which the character expressed her inner life, her thought, her emotion, her need to attain a particular objective. The rhythm and melody of the verbal music depended on the actual vowels and consonants of the individual words, on their meaning, and on the 'ingeniousness' with which the author had used them to express that meaning for the 'person' to whom they were fitted.

A boy playing Rosalind as a girl who disliked 'your brother' but liked 'my sister', who disapproved of their love and wanted to incite Orlando into opposing it, would have a different melody and rhythm from a boy who made the character approve and long for Orlando to recognize her as the girl with whom he fell in love, similarly at first sight, although the circumstances were different. In each case, however, the key words of the figure of *climax* would be emphasized, and the pattern of related words would be heard.

Today, to decide which of these possible interpretations is valid we have to look closely at the whole of the text, working forwards from the beginning and backwards from the end, to see if in fact Shakespeare imagined Rosalind as a person who could begrudge Celia and Oliver their happiness. When we do this we find that the sense of the words in the context of the whole play leaves no room for doubt: she approves and wishes

that she could inspire Orlando into seeing her beneath her disguise as the girl to whom he writes verses. This certainty as to
emotion and objective combines with the pattern of the words
to ensure that every actress who uses them to express the
character's needs will reproduce that pattern and basically the
same rhythm, merely from using her voice in the way that is
natural to her to speak these words for these purposes. Each
actress will still be individual, however; she will not have the
same tones as every other actress; she will merely strive by
means of the same words for the same ends. If this is what happens
today when the structure of the text is taken into account by an
actress, it seems not imprudent to conjecture that it is also what
happened for Elizabethans, especially as the presence of the
author and the fact that the cast were speaking contemporary
language meant that misunderstandings could be eliminated
and alternative readings probably did not exist: if they did, a
definitive ruling could be given. This does not mean for certain,
of course, that such rulings were given. But it is not unreasonable
to conjecture that they might well have been. In any case it
seems reasonable to assume that the lines were spoken in the
only way in which the actor was able to communicate their
meaning, which meaning itself was inseparable in his acting
from the way in which it had been expressed in individual words
in relationship to one another.

The examples considered above are clear; there is no difficulty
in making out their sense. Their poetry is less complex than that
of passages such as Romeo's

> what envious streaks
> Do lace the severing clouds in yonder east;
> Night's candles are burnt out.

The modern actor finds the sense of each individual word clear
enough: but his difficulties begin when he tries to relate each
precisely with a definite emotion and objective within the
character. He has to conquer a tendency to react in a vague, if
powerful, romantic way, in which 'envious', 'lace', and 'night's

candles' are generally, indeterminately 'poetic'. When he has conquered this tendency and realized why each word has been used, that it does what it alone can do here, and that it expresses in its precision much that is relevant for the character and the theme of the play, then he employs the imagery to communicate what is within Romeo. He images for himself the sky in the east where darkness is split by the source of light from which emanate the criss-cross streaks, the lacing. Romeo's resentment of this is expressed in particular by 'envious'; the streaks begrudge him more time with Juliet. The phrase 'night's candles' is used, not as a picturesque example of periphrasis for 'the stars', but because the words allow Romeo to express his regret and resentment that this is not one of the weak, short-burning lights of the night sky, but a brighter light which lasts longer; it is day's lamp against night's candles. The wish that the night could have been longer, the need to stay, the resolution to leave now, are all expressed in 'burnt out', particularly in the word 'out' itself. Romeo's objective is, immediately, to make Juliet realize he must go; his ultimate, or 'super', objective is to live and share his life as Juliet's husband.

I suggest that this is how the Elizabethan actor responded to the lines. The sense of his words decided his emphasis basically; but its full quality developed when he communicated their full meaning for the character. Thus Paulina's objective was important in developing the melody of

> What, sovereign sir,
> I did not well, I meant well.
> (*The Winter's Tale*, v. iii. 2–3.)

The sense of the second line emerges from the patterned relationships: I did—I meant; not well—well. Every actor who wanted to communicate that sense had to use stress, pitch, and changes of length which allowed him to do so, but which also made the relationship of the words 'manifest' to the listener. Two actors speaking this same sense without any emotion or objective beyond that of speaking the sense had the same patterns of stress with equivalent patterns of pitch and length changes. The differences would become greater if they adopted different objectives with consequently differing emotions. Today, one actress might decide that Paulina is selfishly attempting to divert from herself the rage which she fears from Leontes when he discovers how she has concealed his wife from him all these years. A second actress might decide that she is thinking back over all the things which did not turn out as well as she meant them, of the harm done unintentionally; there was the insistence on bringing the baby to Leontes with its consequences; there has been the concealment of the Queen. Now, just before she will reveal his wife to him, Paulina must assure him that every-thing she has done and is about to do is devoid of every trace of malice; nothing but benevolence emanates from her towards him. To play the role this way is to develop a different melody out of the same basic figurative pattern. Again the problem must be solved today by careful scrutiny of the whole text; but the Elizabethan could be given an immediate, definitive ruling. Any two actors today communicating the same emotion, striving for the same objective, will be guided by the figurative pattern of the writing to produce two separate performances of these lines in which much will be identical without infringing on the in-dividual liberty of each respective artist. And as the author was available and the language was contemporary for the Eliza-bethans, it follows that there would be the same kinds of agreements and differences in different performances then.

Writing such as we have been considering allows little, if any, scope for what is called 'interpretation' in the modern theatre. Modern disregard for textual details will allow an actor to create a character whose speaking ignores figurative patterns, parti-cularly figures of words. This obviously was not acceptable to Elizabethans. And as soon as the figures are followed, the actor's concentration on the words will affect his perception of the character, so that he sees where certain of his preconceptions must be abandoned. As the possibilities for interpretation are restricted by the precision and style of the text, it becomes clear that the actor is not really called on to decide between two readings of the same character, but between what are virtually two different characters given the same name. The Paulina who fears the consequences of her actions on her own account is a different person from the woman who wants to protect her friend and master from feeling exposed to hatred. The same woman could not be imagined behaving in two ways in the given circumstances: each type of behaviour demands a separate character-image. I suggest that when the author was alive, when the language was contemporary, and when the ingeniousness of the language was fitted to the person, each actor had the same character-image of the same role, although he had his individual method of embodying it in performance.

The importance of the control exercised by the ingeniousness of the speeches cannot be over-emphasized. Even so simple a pun as Gloucester's 'braz'd' in *King Lear* indicates the quality of the man who is speaking:

> I have so often blush'd to acknowledge him
> that now I am braz'd to 't.
>
> (I. i. 9–10.)

If we gloss 'braz'd' merely as 'hardened', we have a simpler character speaking. But if we give it the Elizabethan sense of 'hardened by fire' we receive a glimpse of the witty roué, quite unabashed by his misdemeanour and the presence of the son begotten by it. Gloucester is now saying that his cheeks have been hardened against shame by the fire of his blushes, and he is enjoying the exercise of wit. He cannot now be played in the opening scene as a sturdy, dullish, honest sort of person who seems reliable enough but has little colour or savour to distinguish him from innumerable other steady and conscientious people. He has to be played as the man who can make this particular quip involving 'blushed–brazed (hardened by fire)'. I find it hard to believe that in the Elizabethan period any actor would have ignored this play upon words: and if he creates his role in terms of it, one element in his character-image is already fixed. But that does not mean that every Elizabethan who played Gloucester spoke these words with the same intonation and pace: it means that the pace and intonation of every actor were what was natural to him to express the same meaning for the character.

When the speeches of an Elizabethan play are ingenious enough and fitted to the person, it is reasonable to conjecture that the Elizabethan actor knew for certain what the words demanded, that he did not unintentionally misunderstand meanings or deliberately or negligently ignore them, and that when the author had worked out a complete character in adequate language, this was what the actor performed. He knew precisely what specific thought, feelings, and desires should be related to each word without vagueness or confusion. Exact explicit sense could be communicated without losing complexity of meaning. And the fact that the scope for interpretation was limited, where it existed, did not by any means prevent a good actor from excelling a mediocre one. Nor were two actors who had essentially the same conception of a role and its performance prevented from individual creation. The acting was not stereotyped merely because the conceptions were the same.

But, obviously, many Elizabethan plays have not been written so well that the actor is guided precisely by the author's complete imagining and utter competence with language. When the author had not done his work properly the actor, then as now, had to do it for him in performance. For instance, in *The Revenger's Tragedy*, Tourneur has not given the Vendice whom he has created in the preceding part of the play a valid reason for falling in with his master's plan and thus tempting and testing his sister and mother. Tourneur's character is a man with room for nothing in his mind but vengeance, who would not divert himself from his main object so wantonly. To play the role convincingly the actor has, and presumably had, to give himself a reason, to behave as if he had caught himself in a trap, and in order to catch the Duke later, must act the pander so despicably now. In fact, in the play as it stands, there is no reason why the Revenger should not lie and report back that his sister refuses. But Tourneur wants to achieve a startling and pathetic theatrical effect without doing the honest work. Similarly, in *The White Devil*, Brachiano is made to murder Isabella because Webster wishes to make his audience react as if, despite all that is done to avoid the clash, the Duke is inevitably made the object of her brother's revenge. The mechanism by which the dramatist achieves or tries to achieve this effect is faulty. First, Isabella averts the clash by taking all the blame for their separation. Brachiano is now free to continue his liaison with his mistress; but as things are he would not be involved in a clash with his brothers-in-law. So, quite unnecessarily, Webster makes him murder his wife; and then their vengeance seeks him out. An actor can give himself quite a number of valid reasons for the murder to play the role convincingly; but these will be his, and not the playwright's.

In Shakespeare's *Antony and Cleopatra*, however, the work has been done as it should be. To avert the threatened clash with Octavius, Antony is easily persuaded to marry Octavia. But once he is married, being the man he is, he cannot be held from Cleopatra. Shakespeare has drawn Antony, Cleopatra, and Octavia completely enough for the outcome to be inevitable. And once Octavia has been deserted there is no possibility of her brother's being satisfied with anything less than full vengeance on Antony. Thus the measure taken to avert a clash proves ironically to have ensured that the clash is inevitable and more violent than it otherwise might have been.

In the first two of these plays it is obvious that the actor is not guided so clearly by his lines as in the third. Shakespeare leaves less possibility, even now, for varying readings of the character than do Tourneur and Webster. This kind of difference between what the actor is given by the good play and by the less good or rank bad, is to be seen in the writing of the 'ingenious speeches' as well as the imagining of 'the persons' to whom they should be fitted. The actor playing Balthasar in *The*

Spanish Tragedy had to do some of his author's work when relating how he has been taken prisoner:

> I think Horatio be my destin'd plague:
> First in his hand he brandished a *sword*,
> And with that *sword* he fiercely waged *war*,
> And in that *war* he gave me dangerous *wounds*,
> And by those *wounds* he forced me to *yield*,
> And by my *yielding*, I became his slave.
>
> (II. i. 118–23.)

In his need to create the pattern of climax, Kyd has put into Balthasar's mouth words which certainly attain that end, but which do not express exactly what he intended also to imagine the character would have within him. Until Balthasar remembers how he was wounded, the account is imprecise: *sword* and *war* have to be used for the pattern, but they do not express precisely what the actor must imagine as having happened. He must remember how Horatio caught sight of him, waved his sword aggressively at him, cut his way through the fighting (not 'fiercely waged war'). But when the player reaches 'gave me dangerous wounds' he no longer has to think his own thoughts while articulating Kyd's words. Now these can each be related precisely to what is thought, felt, and wanted in the person of the represented character. In fact, Kyd's speech lacks 'ingeniousness' as well as not being fitted to the person. The actor had to improve it in both these respects.

But Claudius' lines of false rejoicing as he pretends to anticipate Hamlet's triumph are ingenious and fitted to the person:

> Let the kettle to the *trumpet* speak,
> The *trumpet* to the *cannoneer* without,
> The *cannons* to the *heavens*, the *heaven* to earth,
> 'Now the King drinks to Hamlet'.
>
> (V. ii. 267–70.)

Here the Elizabethan actor did not have the same need to imagine for himself. What the character has in mind is clear because the words are used precisely for his purposes as well as to create an ingenious pattern.

We can see the same distinction between the well-written and the slovenly written in other aspects of Elizabethan dramatic writing: these also present the actor with a clearly and completely-worked-out character, or an incomplete or confused substitute respectively. With the latter he had to cover up the writer's failure by using his own imagination; he acted, not by performing the words in his role, but by ignoring them to a large extent; he had to give his own meaning while articulating them. I think it safe to conjecture that when *The Malcontent* was performed in the Jacobean theatre (?1600–?1604), the actor playing Malevole managed to conceal from his audience the very bad writing of:

> Duke, I'll torment thee now: my just revenge
> From thee than crown a richer gem shall part:
> Beneath God naught's so dear as a calm heart.
>
> (I. iii. 198–200.)

The 'ingeniousness' at which the author was aiming included both the placing of a *sententia* in the character's mouth and the writing of it in couplets, in addition to the usual matters of imagining a person who would express such sentiments at this point and of writing lucid and melodious verse. Marston's actor was given the *sententia* and a valid reason as the character for speaking its sentiments here: but the couplet is bad, and the verse neither lucid nor melodious. He had to think and communicate clearly what Marston has expressed badly in the tortuous syntax of 'From thee than crown a richer gem shall part'; and his voice would then have a melody which could come only from deliberately (and in this case justifiably) ignoring what he was given to speak. Earlier in the same speech his action could give men like Baker pleasure simply by communicating the meaning and quality of:

> Distemperance rob thy sleep!
> The heart's disquiet is revenge most deep.
>
> (185–6.)[1]

Now the lines are precise enough to guide an actor in his playing; they restrict the possibilities of interpretation.

[1] Ed. Brooke and Paradise, p. 368.

But there was even less scope and more guidance for the boy playing Lady Macbeth as she begins to realize exactly what sort of a situation she has involved herself and her husband in:

> Nought's had, all's spent,
> Where our desire is got without content.
> 'Tis safer to be that which we destroy,
> Than by destruction dwell in doubtful joy.
>
> (III. ii. 47.)

Sir Michael Redgrave's comment on the first two lines of this passage is a useful illustration of the way in which 'interpretation' of a Shakespearian role develops today: 'The couplet I have just quoted can, after all, be perfectly well read in the character of the greedy ambitious woman who is never satisfied', without any hint of her eventual breakdown.[1] This is true if the lines are abstracted from their context; but in it they are followed by the second couplet which states explicitly that she has found from experience that she is not safe. She was once certain that the murder done in her way would bring no danger. In these words she recognizes that it has turned out differently, that she dwells without safety in 'doubtful joy'; and 'doubtful' here has the sense of 'fearful' as well as our modern 'uncertain'. In the speech as a whole Lady Macbeth expresses more than the greed of an unsatisfied, ambitious woman: this can be made the meaning of the first two lines only if the next two are ignored. Today, actress and director must examine every word carefully if a misleading 'interpretation' is to be avoided. I do not believe that an Elizabethan would have permitted himself, or have been permitted, to detach the earlier couplet from the one into which it leads, not only so far as style is concerned, but as an expression of what takes place within the character. Shakespeare's use of words is so precise that to pay attention to them all in this case is to find guidance in playing the role.

Some pre-Restoration dramatists have admitted that in fact the actors covered up their defects. Webster apologized to The

[1] 'Shakespeare and the Actors', in *Talking of Shakespeare*, ed. J. Garrett (1954), pp. 135 f.

Judicious Reader of *The Devil's Law-case*: 'I am so far from praising myself, that I have not given way to divers of my friends, whose unbegged commendatory verses offered themselves to do me service in the front of this poem. A great part of the grace of this (I confess) lay in action: yet can no action ever be gracious, where the decency of the language and the ingenious structure of the scene arrive not to make up a perfect harmony.'[1] Certainly he was right in saying that the acting gave grace to his play; but the skill of innumerable actors of the eighteenth and nineteenth centuries attests to the fact that action can be gracious without decency of language and the ingenious structure of the scene. The most famous example is probably that of Irving, who took such trash as *The Bells* and, by doing the author's work himself on the stage, made it seem a play of consequence.

Webster insists, however, that although a bad play can be performed so well that it seems good, when a reader has the opportunity of reading it, all that was disguised by the acting is now revealed in its true quality. And so he apologizes for *The White Devil*, saying that it was written to be played before the incapable multitude: 'Willingly and not ignorantly in this kind have I defaulted.'[2] Massinger was praised (quite untruly, in my opinion) by his admirers for writing plays which did not rely on the actor to amend their deficiencies:

> Action gives many poems right to live,
> This piece gave life to action; and will give
> For state and language, in each change of age,
> To time, delight; and honour to the stage.[3]

His *Emperor of the East* was declared to be a play which

> shall live long,
> Not die as soon as passed the actor's tongue.[4]

---

[1] Works, ed. F. L. Lucas (1927), ii. 236.

[2] Ed. Symonds, p. 3.

[3] John Ford, 'To the deserving Memory of this Worthy Work', prefixed to Massinger, *The Great Duke of Florence* (1636), sig. A4ᵛ.

[4] (1632), sig. A4ʳ.

When *Parisitaster, or The Fawn* went to the press in 1606, Marston was conscious that the play's success in performance was due to the acting rather than the quality of his 'ingenious' writing: 'If any shall wonder why I print a comedy, whose life rests much in the actor's voice, let such know that it cannot avoid publishing. Let it therefore stand with good excuse, that I have been my own setter out.' He promises to write a tragedy 'which shall abide the most curious perusal'. This comedy must be excused by the admission that 'comedies are writ to be spoken, not read. Remember the life of these things consists in action'.[1]

Marston had already made a similar apology when *The Malcontent* was published in 1604, regretting 'that scenes invented merely to be spoken, should be enforcively published to be read'. He hoped that 'the unhandsome shape which this trifle in reading presents may be pardoned for the pleasure it once afforded you when it was presented with the soul of lively action'.[2]

Plays of this and lesser quality obviously depended on the actor creating a complete character and giving music and poetry where the author had not done his own work competently. This means that the original actor of a role had more scope for interpretation; but there is little evidence to tell us what happened once the part had been set. It is impossible to be sure whether pre-Restoration custom and prejudice demanded that the original interpretation must be adhered to, or whether each succeeding player of the role developed its basic conception in his own way. In any case, variations in the quality of the writing within one particular play may well have meant that in some scenes there was less need for, and less possibility of, interpretation.

The Elizabethan practice of acting for wagers might be taken as showing that it was possible to measure individual performances against a standard comparable to that which can be applied to musical performances today. In music, detailed and specific comparisons can be made between one performance and another; and when two soloists are inspired by the same conception, and aiming at the same goal, there is still scope for individuality to

[1] Sig. A2ʳ, A2ᵛ.　　　[2] Sig. A4ʳ.

be expressed as well as for more superficial technical skill to be exhibited. The Elizabethan custom of backing one player against another in the same role was well established. According to the *Henslowe Papers* a certain 'W.P.' accepted a wager from 'a party affected to other actors' and backed Edward Alleyn to outshine them in any play in which Bentley or Knell had appeared.[1] In *Ratseis Ghost* (1605) Ratsey urges a likely actor to leave the countryside for London: 'I durst venture all the money in my purse on thy head, to play Hamlet with him Burbage for a wager.'[2] In his *Jests to Make You Merry* (1607), Dekker tells of a 'pair of players growing into an emulous contention of one another's worth, refused to put themselves to a day of hearing (as any players would have done), but stood only upon their good parts'. The same writer tells a gallant how to behave in a tavern: 'let any hook draw you either to a fencer's supper, or to a player's that acts such a part for a wager'.[3] William Fennor boasted to John Taylor:

> And let me tell thee this to calm thy rage,
> I challenged Kendall on the Fortune stage;
> And he did promise 'fore an audience
> For to oppose me.[4]

In the Epilogue to *The Jew of Malta*, spoken at the Cockpit by William Perkins, playing Barabas, we can read:

> Nor think that this day any prize was play'd,
> Here were no bets at all, no wagers laid.[5]

Perhaps amateurs acted for wagers, too, if we can rely on the Citizen's boast in *The Knight of the Burning Pestle* (Prologue), that Ralph

> should have play'd Jeronimo
> With a shoe-maker for a wager.

I am disposed to interpret this evidence of acting for wagers

---

[1] Ed. W. W. Greg, p. 32.   [2] Sig. B1ʳ.
[3] Sig. B4ʳ; and *Gull's Hornbook* (1609), sig. F2ᵛ.
[4] See Chambers, *The Elizabethan Stage*, ii. 191.   [5] Sig. A4ᵛ.

as suggesting the possibility that a standard existed against which individual performances could be measured. With really 'ingenious speeches' fitted to a completely-worked-out character, meaning, music, character-image, and performance of the nuances of literary style were inseparable. A good player enabled his audience to relate character in action to the existence of a literary text without seeming any less the person he represented: in actual fact, the seeming was greater rather than less. Two performances could be very near to one another in certain respects without being slavish imitations of one another or of any 'original'. The same figure of words or of sentence could be heard expressing the same thought, emotion, and desire for the same character in the same situation, yet each speaker would not speak in exactly the same tones, nor would they be of the same duration and intensity. Movement, appearance, gesture would be like and unlike one another in the same manner.

On the other hand, it must be conceded that the evidence need not be interpreted in this way. To decide a wager, different conceptions as well as differing details of 'action' could have been compared. It seems to me that this was less possible with well-written, fully developed plays than with those such as *The Malcontent* and *The White Devil*. With these there was obviously more possibility of interpreting as this is practised today.

If this was the case, we must assume the possibility of two attitudes to performance: one relating to really 'ingenious' speeches where the player is controlled more by the way the words have been written, the other to inferior plays where the actor has to do the author's work. With these there is no doubt that, in Gainsford's words, 'player was ever the life of dead poesy'.[1] The player had to do what Irving did so often with the badly written, inadequately developed romantic melodrama of the nineteenth century. For instance, he made the crudely drawn burgomaster of *The Bells* into a sensitive, conscience-racked victim of his own crime. All of which was very fine; but as one critic said, such a man would never have committed the murder

[1] T. Gainsford, *The Rich Cabinet* (1616), sig. Q4^{r}.

in the first place.[1] This did not matter when Irving was conceal-
ing the play's weakness with his strengths in performance; but
it became obvious to anyone who read the script or thought about
the plot in cold blood afterwards. Irving could hide the weaknesses
of inferior plays. I suggest that this was true of Elizabethan
actors with lesser plays, too; but I doubt if they changed the
better ones.

The rules to which the actors conformed were inherent in the
quality of the writing. As I have already pointed out, the actor
who omitted to make manifest the figure 'surcease, success' is
giving an incomplete performance of Macbeth as a character;
his failure on both counts is apparent to an audience capable of
noticing the likeness in sound and the actor's neglect of it.
Elizabethan actors often acted to audiences of this capacity. With
such writing and on such occasions the scope for interpretation
was limited; but the players were free as creative artists, without
the least compulsion towards slavish, stereotyped imitation.

Whatever the truth may be as to interpreting roles, I am
certain that in every case, and whatever the interpretation, the
actor was identified. If we adopt the terminology of the futile
and really quite unnecessary controversy on the subject, the
Elizabethan player was always what Harbage calls natural, and
never what he calls formal. The term 'natural' is really too vague
in this context; but we are probably justified in using it in that
whatever formality was involved, however unrealistic his lines
or other elements of dramatic technique, the actor still appeared
'the very man' on the stage; he still used tones, facial expressions,
movement which were natural to him to communicate the inner
life of the person he represented.

There is another problem, however, to which so certain an
answer cannot be given. It is difficult to be sure how far Elizabethan performance created an 'individualized' and how far
what used to be called an 'idealized' character on the stage. By
individualized is meant the representation of individual external

---

[1] *The Athenaeum* (1892), ii. 458. See also the present writer's *The Tragic Actor*,
pp. 366 f.

mannerisms, idiosyncratic expressions of personality by which a real human being can be recognized before he speaks. An individualized representation of Macbeth might show the gradual development of a facial or bodily twitch as a result of the mounting strain of forcing himself to seem innocent and unconcerned when all the time he suffers increasing terror of being recognized for what he is. Fearful of exposure, longing not to be seen by every eye, he makes himself look people in the face. And the twitch betrays his tension.

A more idealized presentation would portray the same conflict between what he would like to do and what he must do, between terrified reality and seeming confidence, but without the actor having included this idiosyncrasy in his character-image. The role has been written without any indication of such things and it can be played to perfection without them. But there is no certainty that it was played in the idealized rather than the individualized way in the Elizabethan theatre.

Eighteenth-century actors, even Garrick and his school, tended to the idealized presentation of character, especially in tragedy.[1] Edmund Kean shows some tendency to individualization; but the individualized performance really developed in the art of Macready and Charles Kean until it dominated the English stage.[2] The balance of individualized and idealized elements in a performance can be adjusted so subtly, however, that Irving and Ellen Terry now seem individualized, contrasted with earlier players, yet appeared idealized to their contemporaries when contrasted with developments taking place in the eighteen nineties.[3] Moreover, when we consider the question of idealization we should remember that comedy probably tended to be more individualized than tragedy on the Elizabethan stage.

To some extent we can deduce the answer to our problem from the author's style which reveals in its formality the way in which he is idealizing rather than individualizing the character as he imagines it. The idealized character is no less an individual, but

---

[1] *The Tragic Actor*, pp. 88 ff., 103, 109, 112 ff., 125 f., 153.
[2] Ibid., pp. 264 ff.   [3] Ibid., pp. 379 f., 381.

the style of his utterances controls the style of performance. The opening speeches of *The Merchant of Venice* all betoken idealized characters; yet from the first Antonio, Salerio, and Solanio are differentiated as individuals. Solanio speaks lines which insist on a conception of him as a more restless, quicker, less dignified sort of person than Salerio, whose rhythms and vocabulary belong to a calmer, solider personage. The rhythm is expressed in a different conception of physique and psychology in each case, yet there is no suggestion that any particular quirk or mannerism must enter into performing either.[1] To play either with individualized mannerism would not necessarily be wrong, however, provided it were possible to do so without doing violence to Shakespeare's style. Modern actors tend to individualize their presentations of Shakespeare's roles where he seems to have imagined them only as fully as is necessary for development in the action. Old Siward will receive individualized characteristics to give him superficial interest as a human being, while Banquo, the depth of whose character is more immediately apparent, tends to be played in a more idealized manner. But what happened before 1642 is uncertain. Style is the nearest thing to a sure guide.

The style or 'ingeniousness' of the speeches fitted to the persons must have affected the acting. Greater formality of literary style meant a greater element of formality in performance, but without making the acting any less natural. It was still not what modern academic writers on the subject call formal. To understand how formality and naturalness can be fused in a performance which presents a character seeming to be the very man, we need to consider more closely the complexities of the psychological and imaginative state known as being identified with the character. An identified actor does not suffer an hallucination. One part of his consciousness thinks, feels, and wants as if he were the character he is playing. But other parts know clearly that he is not the character, that he is a particular actor at a particular time in a particular place, playing to a

[1] My attention was called to these points by Duncan Ross.

particular audience. He is conscious of the sensations which he, the actor, experiences physically and mentally as a result of playing the character. He is conscious of the quality of the play itself, of individual speeches, or their style, as a whole and in individual lines. While behaving as if he were the character, the actor can still respond as an actor to the dramatist's art, to the style of the lines, recognizing their formality or lack of it. All these elements of his attention are mixed in the right proportions and integrated as a result of his preparation, when he might have spent a considerable time perfecting the vocal technique which now allows him to communicate truthfully an emotion felt by the character and expressed by the author in formal verse. The fact that conscious art has gone into the performance, and that he is conscious of employing the technique successfully, does not make him any the less identified or his acting any the less natural. It was failure to realize this that misled Keats into thinking Edmund Kean to be a spontaneous actor, delivering himself up 'to the instant feeling, without a shadow of a thought about anything else'. In fact, as Hazlitt recognized, Kean's acting was 'throughout elaborate and systematic, instead of being loose, off-hand and accidental'. Lewes notes that he was able to act his parts 'with the precision of a singer who has thoroughly learned his air'. Vandenhoff described him in rehearsal as accurately counting 'the number of steps he had to take before reaching a certain spot, or before uttering a certain word; these steps were justly regarded by him as part of the mechanism which could no more be neglected than the accompaniment to an air could be neglected by the singer'. The accent and rhythm of his 'Blood, Iago; blood, blood!' were always the same, 'as a Tamberlik may deliver the C from the chest with more sonority one night than another, but always delivers it from the chest and never from the head'.[1]

I believe that the elements of the Elizabethan actor's 'absorbed attention' were so integrated that he remained identified, never came out of character and succeeded in suiting the formality of

[1] *The Tragic Actor*, pp. 269 ff.

the author's style.[1] It was not a matter of playing a formal passage 'formally' and a less formal one 'naturally'. However unrealistic or formal the style of a speech might be, that did not mean that it was played with anything but a natural use of voice, face, and gesture. Both realistic and unrealistic dramatic dialogue demanded from the actor voice, appearance, and movement natural to him to communicate what was going on within him as if he were the person represented. Variations in the realism or in the complexity of poetic quality did not detract from the naturalness with which thought, emotion, and desire were communicated. This naturalness was blended with the other elements in the actor's attention, one of which was a response to the formality of the lines. But there was never, it seems to me, an abrupt change, or even a gradual change from wholly 'formal' to the kind of individualistic truth ignoring the style of the lines which can be met with on modern stages. Nor was there a mixture of what Harbage calls 'formal' with what he calls 'natural'. The change from blank verse to couplet in the first scene of *King Lear* must have affected the style of acting, but the actors were no less identified, and seemed no less the persons represented, as if they had come to life. As the Elizabethan actor responded to variations in the style of his lines, so the style of his performance varied. Rhythm, tempo of speech and movement, and melody of speech would have been affected by stylistic variations, but there would still have remained untouched the essential naturalness of behaviour, which was that of such a person communicating what was within him in the circumstances of the action.

Where a dramatist had imagined in terms of human character the actor could do justice to poetic passages without losing his identification. The modern actor is torn two ways by a line such as the First Murderer's 'The west yet glimmers with some streaks of day', because it is a famous 'poetic' statement and it is put in the mouth of a ruthless desperado concerned not with the beauties of the evening but with revenge. I do not think that

---

[1] I am indebted to Duncan Ross for the term 'absorbed attention' to describe the actor's complex awareness of himself and his role.

the Elizabethan actor spoke this line as a beautiful description of the sky, coming out of his character to do so, but that he imagined himself taking up position to kill Banquo, afraid for the moment that he might be too late. Macbeth has insisted the murder must be secret, so the murderers dare not come until it is dark enough for concealment. But if it has got too dark, their prey will already have made his way past this spot. And so, after his first anxiety, the Murderer notices with satisfaction that it is not completely dark, that they have come unnoticed, and they are in time. This is why he takes the trouble to describe the sky. When a modern actor plays the line with this objective, as if he actually saw the sky, it is effective as description and as communication of the needs of the character. There is no reason to believe that anything else happened in Shakespeare's day.

It is misleading to talk of an Elizabethan acting style: the style of an Elizabethan actor at any particular moment was determined by that of the words he was acting; and as that fluctuated so did his acting. It is equally misleading to talk generally of the style of a particular play or writer. Within what we may generally describe as a writer's style are innumerable variations. I have already remarked on the variations in style of the first scene of *King Lear*; not only in Shakespeare but in the other pre-Restoration writers we can find changes of style from line to line which demanded and received from the actor a corresponding change in his acting without in any way making him seem any less the actual person he was representing. Just as he responded to *sententia* when it occurred in couplet in a play written for the most part in blank verse and prose, so he responded to couplet at the end of act or scene, or as we find it in so many of the speeches in Heywood's *A Woman Killed With Kindness*. In the scene of Sir Charles's arrest he has blank verse speeches ending in couplet:

> her silver brow,
> That never tasted a rough winter's blast
> Without a mask or fan, doth with a grace
> Defy cold winter, and his storms outface.   (III. i. 40-43.)

And Susan, alone after her brother's departure for prison and before Acton and Maltby come upon her, laments:

> My heart's so harden'd with the frost of grief,
> Death cannot pierce it through.—Tyrant too fell!
> So lead the fiends condemned souls to hell.
>
> (III. i. 73–75.)[1]

In each case the actor's 'absorbed attention' includes an appreciation of the changes of style as well as a responding to the situation as if really the person involved.

Departures from realism such as monologue and aside did not make the actor communicate thought, emotion, and desire any less naturally. A monologue in which the audience was directly addressed need not have meant that the actor was no longer identified any more than it does today. The actor nowadays remains in character; he brings the audience differently into what Stanislavski calls his 'circle of concentration',[2] behaving as if he were the character talking to the audience. Essentially there is no difference imaginatively between behaving as if he were the actual person talking to other 'persons of the drama' and behaving as if he were that person talking to an audience; he is still identified. I know of no reason for assuming that the Elizabethan practice should have been different.

Similarly the Elizabethan actor had no reason to be anything but identified and to behave just as if he were the actual person represented when he spoke asides. Others on the stage continued to behave as if they had not heard him; of course they would have to wait until he finished speaking before taking up the dialogue again; but that meant nothing essentially different from what happens in any case when an identified actor waits for his cue. A part of his attention acknowledges the fact that he is performing; another part responds, exactly as if the imaginary character, to what has been said or done, and speaks the author's lines because of the character's need to use them. When the character is given a soliloquy which we can interpret as an

---

[1] Ed. Brooke and Paradise, p. 306.
[2] See D. Magarshack, op. cit., pp. 40 f.

unrealistic representation of silent thoughts, the actor does not have to be less identified: again there is a slightly different blending of the elements of his attention, but he uses voice, face, and gesture to communicate what the character thinks, feels, and wants. He is not now trying to make an impact on somebody else in the play, but he still has his objective, and he still communicates his will to attain it. There are times when Elizabethan dramatists have given actors speeches which we moderns would like to interpret as representing silent thought, but which obviously could be overheard by an eavesdropper. Here, again, although the speech is unrealistic, it demands from the identified actor that he use voice, face, and gesture to express naturally what he has within, still looking and sounding as if he were the very man.

It is not possible to be sure of many details of actual performance, how actors stood in relation to one another when speaking dialogue, how they were grouped. Some evidence is provided by John Stephens's character of *A Common Player*, but it will bear contradictory interpretations:

> When he doth hold conference upon the stage, and should look directly in his fellow's face, he turns about his voice into the assembly for applause-sake, like a trumpeter in the fields, that shifts places to get an echo.[1]

Stephens may be attacking a general habit, shared even by good actors, of speaking out front instead of simulating dialogue with superficial realism; he may be attacking those bad actors whose custom this was, a custom not shared by their betters; or he may be attacking the practice of all actors at certain moments in performance, when, despite the fact that they were speaking dialogue, the most effective way of communicating to the audience was to face front instead of one another.

Some speeches which seem at first sight to be dialogue in Elizabethan plays can be recognized on further examination as not representing speech between the characters. There are a

---

[1] *Essays and Characters* (1615), p. 297.

number of these in the scene in *The Third Part of Henry VI* (II. v)
in which the King stands by while a father discovers he has
killed his own son, and a son that he has killed his father. Similar
to these are such speeches as Cleopatra's apostrophe to the
absent Antony ('Think on me' (I. v)) and Octavius' evocation of
the Antony whom he remembers and admires:

> at thy heel
> Did famine follow, whom thou fought'st against
> (Though daintily brought up) with patience more
> Than savages could suffer.
>
> (I. iv. 58–61.)

In such cases it is likely that the actor faced his audience, still in
character, and without directly addressing them, communicated
to them naturally what was within the character.

It is possible that there were times when passages of dialogue
were performed in a similar manner. I found at the Mermaid
Theatre at St. John's Wood and in the Royal Exchange from
1951 to 1953 that actors could successfully face their audience and
give to the spectators when speaking dialogue what is normally
given to the other person or persons to whom the words are
addressed. Such acting was still not formal; the actor was still
identified, he still sounded and looked as such a man would in the
circumstances; his voice sounded natural, his appearance was
also natural. During the course of a whole performance there
would be innumerable changes of focus, always still in character,
with one part of a speech being directed at one part of the house,
another at another. In 1951 Horatio started speaking to his
companions as he gave the explanation of the warlike prepara-
tions, but soon turned from them and spoke into the auditorium,
so that the spectators saw him exactly as he would have appeared
to another person to whom he was speaking dialogue. As I have
already observed, our modern audiences perceived nothing unnatural or 'formal'. If such variations in positioning and 'attack'
allowed the actors to seem natural and lifelike in the middle of
this century to an audience half-expecting unusual posture and
gesticulation, there is every reason to conjecture that the same

sort of behaviour by Elizabethan actors seemed equally natural and lifelike to their contemporaries.

I suggest that the Elizabethan always spoke or aimed at speaking every speech as if it were essential for the character to speak it at that particular moment. This was not altered by the fact that the dramatist might be using the speech for other purposes at the same time. An actor who recognized these other purposes still had to act the speech as if he were the person represented, had to find this person's reason for speaking, and make it his own. The opening of *Cymbeline* makes use of the First Gentleman to give an exposition of the facts of the situation, an introduction to some of the characters, and to interest the audience, partly by making them wonder whether events and people are exactly as he sees them. But the actor has, and had, to identify himself with a man who cannot contain himself, who must pour out what he feels about all that has been happening, who wants to share with the Second Gentleman his certainty of the injustice done, who wants to hear someone agree with him about Imogen, Posthumous, the wicked Queen, her stupid son, the deceived King, and who is longing for the time when the evil will be unmasked, when Cymbeline's eyes have been opened, and when the Princess and her husband come into their own again. When a modern actor plays the role in this way he seems natural, his needs as the character hold the audience, who also receive the facts which the author puts into his exposition. I suggest that this was the Elizabethan method of dealing with the problem as well.

To some extent a knowledge of the details of Elizabethan behaviour off the stage can guide us as to the practice of the actors on it. Many elements of Tudor and Stuart social behaviour would seem 'formal' or 'symbolic' to us; courtesies, the removing of headgear, remaining uncovered, the giving and taking of hands, arms, kisses, and embraces could obviously involve a symbolic element at particular moments; but where we might regard these things as deliberately unusual, the original audiences probably reacted as we do to the extra significance of the giving or rejection of a hand to be shaken. Formalities of social life which preserved distinctions of rank must have been repeated on the stage; subjects would be shown on one knee or both, in accordance with decorum off the stage. At a particular moment neglect to observe or the observing of such a custom might have special significance, as when Goneril and Regan and their retinues cease to give Lear the deference due to a king, when Oswald dares to look him full in the eyes and defy him, and, on the other hand, when Kent recognizes his authority, and when Cordelia and her retinue serve him on their knees.

A problem is presented by descriptions given in the text by one person of another's appearance or behaviour. Sometimes a modern historian of the theatre doubts whether it was possible for the Player in *Hamlet* actually to grow pale as the Prince describes him. But changes of colour, like tears, smiles, frowns, and an appearance of distraction, are possible with an identified actor, imagining strongly what it would be like if he were the character. There are other descriptions of persons behaving in ways which are all physically possible, but which may not have actually taken place on the stage; the descriptions might have been spoken for exactly that reason, so that the audience would respond as if seeing what is described. We may wonder whether an Elizabethan actor ever played Wolsey as he is described by Norfolk:

> Some strange commotion
> Is in his brain: he bites his lip and starts,
> Stops on a sudden, looks upon the ground,
> Then lays his finger on his temple; straight
> Springs out into fast gait; then stops again,
> Strikes his breast hard; and anon he casts
> His eye against the moon. In most strange postures
> We have seen him set himself.
> (*King Henry VIII*, III. ii. 112–19.)

We can be sure, I think, that Henry was played frowning in an 'aspect of terror' at Cranmer in Act V, Sc. i, as the stage-direction actually calls for this in Act III, Sc. ii, when the King exits '*frowning upon the Cardinal*'.[1] But it may still be doubted by some that any actor in *Henry V* really showed in face and body what is described in the King's lines before Harfleur (III. i. 6–17). Did Mowbray really spit at Bolingbroke on the line, 'I do defy him and I spit at him' (*Richard II*, I. i. 60) when the play was performed on an Elizabethan stage? The actor may well have shown his contempt by spitting, as only in comparatively recent times has spitting in public been given up for social and sanitary reasons. While it is obvious that the boy went through the motion of washing his hands when he played Lady Macbeth, it is not clear whether the Elizabethan actors addressed by Richard actually did what he describes, or whether he is speaking figuratively:

> Though some of you, with Pilate, wash your hands,
> Showing an outward pity.
>
> (IV. i. 239–40.)

But I am inclined to believe that the boy playing Imogen wrung his hands as described by Bulwer[2] (see 'Ploro', C in Fig. 2), when Belarius commented:

> He wrings at some distress.
> (*Cymbeline*, III. vi. 78.)

Such things are described as normal in renaissance books on gesture, physiology, physiognomy, painting, and psychology; they are to be seen in the sculpture, painting, and engraving of the age. But that does not mean that we can be sure they were done on the stage. Each case has to be considered separately. I find it impossible to believe that Hamlet did not sigh, and that his arms were not crossed. Similarly, I assume that an actor of Macduff before 1642 pulled his hat over his brows, both because it appears so from the text, and because it was a normal way of expressing self-isolation into personal troubles, and one which seemed natural to contemporaries. I think we may assume that an identified actor may have behaved in the way which the text

---

[1] The First Folio contains this stage direction.
[2] *Chirol.*, pp. 28 f.

describes when this allowed him to communicate naturally and forcefully, and when social custom did not inhibit him.

For Baker and Elizabethans like him, the greatest pleasure of performance came from the 'action' because it added sound of voice and appearance of face and body to the other pleasures of a dramatist's writing. Performance gave the play simultaneously as literature and imagined incident in which place and character were represented by stage and actor respectively. But obviously there was more to performance than acting: there was pageantry, fencing, fighting, music, and singing. There was the colour of processions, of grouping, of clothing and of curtains, hangings, painted properties, and decoration.

These were not in conflict with the actor's performance. As his acting presented an imaginary character in a blending of unrealistic and realistic elements, so the stage, the properties, the movements and groupings upon it, presented imaginary places and incidents with an equivalent blending of much that was realistic and much that was not. And in each case, in that of the acting, and in that of the stage and its properties, the audience was able to imagine a place, a person, an incident as if it were real, while knowing it to be represented. In each case success came from players imagining themselves the very persons in a specific place and on a specific occasion. A door which was a permanent part of the stage structure was obviously more realistic than a post representing a tree; but the door was accepted as representing the gate of a castle or city, as the post was accepted as representing a tree, simply because each was treated as such by the actors. When they behaved as if they were the imaginary characters come to life, a scene played in broad daylight could represent one taking place in the dark, and was imagined as such by the audience. To speak blank verse did not mean to behave unnaturally or not in a very lifelike manner; this was true also of behaving in daylight as if in darkness. The actors on the stage in daylight imagined themselves on a platform before the castle of Elsinore at night in Denmark. They imagined themselves terrified of another actor behaving as if he were the Ghost; they attempted to stop and strike at a substantial figure which evaded them, whereupon they behaved as if it had been insubstantial and had vanished into the air, despite the fact that it had gone down a trap-door, or merely off through a stage-door.

For the actors to do such things, and for the audience to respond to them, was not a matter of offering and accepting conventions in place of realistic imitation of reality. The audience imagined darkness when an actor came on the stage with a lantern, not because this was a convention, but because he held it as if he really needed it to see where and with whom he was standing. A real actor on a real chair represented an imaginary person on an imaginary chair; a real actor on a real upper-stage represented an imaginary person on the imaginary walls of a town. When the play succeeded, the audience imagined it as involving imaginary persons, incidents, and places which evoked a response as if they were really the things represented. It did not matter whether the imaginary was represented realistically or unrealistically, so long as it was accepted and treated as if it were not imaginary by the actors. Of late years there have been revolutionary conjectures as to the conditions of performance and the facts of stage architecture in the Elizabethan period.[1] It is becoming apparent that in some ways properties and stage structures were more realistic than used to be thought possible. On the other hand it is also becoming clear that many unrealistic elements of medieval staging persisted as late as the seventeenth century. Professor Wickham has shown that canvas houses were still used, and that the theatres shared with the street pageants the practice of representing a town or city by means of a small canvas and framework castle appropriately painted.[2] The audience

---

[1] See the following: J. C. Adams, *The Globe Playhouse* (1942); W. A. Armstrong, *The Elizabethan Private Theatres* (1958); C. W. Hodges, *The Globe Restored* (1953); L. Hotson, *The First Night of Twelfth Night* (1954), *Shakespeare's Wooden O* (1959); A. M. Nagler, *Shakespeare's Stage* (1958); A. Nicoll, ed., *Shakespeare Survey (The Theatre)* (1959); R. Southern, *The Open Stage* (1953); G. W. Wickham, *Early English Stages 1300–1660*, Vol. I (1959); F. P. Wilson, 'The Elizabethan Theatre', *Neophilologus* (1955).

[2] *Early English Stages, 1300–1660*, Vol. II, 1576–1660, Part I (1963), pp. 285 ff.

accepted this not as the result of a convention, but because the actors imagined it to be really what it represented, and behaved as if it were.

If we take into account the basic fact that the Elizabethan stage was a place on which actors behaved as if in a specific location, which sometimes helped them and probably never hindered them, it becomes quite plausible that there were times and places in which performers might have been surrounded by their audience, as on an arena stage today. Whether this happened or not is a matter to be decided by historians of theatre architecture and performance; but in making that decision there is no justification for arguing that the arena of this sort would not have been tolerated by the audience. It was possible to act on the main stage with actors entering and leaving through groups of spectators sitting with their backs to the tiring house wall. And there is no artistic reason to object to the conjecture that the occupants of the upper stage in the De Witt drawing were spectators. When our production of the first scene of *Hamlet* was performed for the second time in 1951 at the Mermaid Theatre in St. John's Wood, it was impossible to accommodate all our audience in the auditorium. I therefore advised Mr. and Mrs. Miles to allow spectators to stand in the upper stage. Their presence in modern clothing did not interfere with the response of the rest of the audience below; and a number of them assured me that they were not conscious of any difficulty themselves as they watched from above. This does not prove that spectators watched from the upper stage in the Elizabethan theatre, but that it would have been possible for them to enjoy a performance from this part of the house, and without spoiling the enjoyment of the rest of the audience.

It seems safe to assume that, for many members of most audiences, performance was enjoyable because it gave them the play which they could read and added to it the actors' 'action'. Obviously we cannot claim that this was true of all playgoers. The quality of the acting varied from theatre to theatre as well as the quality of the play; and places such as the Red Bull offered crude spectacle and 'inexplicable dumbshow' rather than 'that gracefulness of action' which Baker found the greatest pleasure of a play. Moreover, much as we may validly talk of the Elizabethan response as an aesthetic experience, a conscious response to what was acknowledgedly a work of art, there must have been playgoers to whose response this does not apply at all. Then, as now, and in the eighteenth and nineteenth centuries there must have been people who were so moved as to take the imaginary persons for real. Leaving it to psychologists and practitioners of aesthetics to decide whether this response is in any way akin to hallucination rather than to the imagining of a work of art, we can be sure that it involved imagining very strongly as the result of the natural, lifelike acting on the stage.

Where the audience found much of its enjoyment in the fighting, fencing, acrobatics, horse-play, the dancing, the processions, and the dressing of the cast, what brought people to the theatre was the fact that all these elements were integrated in the presentation of a play. The difference between the play and the individual elements of this kind involved in its performance lies essentially in its words: story can be told and character represented without words, but the Elizabethan play is a story told in words and involves characters represented by actors speaking them. From the words given him to speak, the Elizabethan actor created character; he and his fellows who were engaged in the same activity imagined, and led their audiences to imagine, incidents linked in a developing plot, with the implications becoming apparent; the performance was given in articulate sound and purposive movement. Where the play was well written the actor's inspiration came wholly from the words; they mattered most in the theatre as in reading. Acting a badly written play he added meaning and beauty which the author had failed to give.

The acting was what was required by the drama and the audiences. To some men it gave more of an experience of poetry than they could find for themselves when reading. Others, such as Baker, found in the acting everything which was present for them in reading. An Elizabethan playgoer, capable of responding sensitively to a play when he read it, could expect at least as rich an experience of the play as a poem when watching and listening to the actors performing it in the theatre. His experience of the play as poem arose out of his reacting to the actors as if they were the very persons whom they represented; it also arose out of their speaking with due attention to the literary quality of their lines. For actors and audience the two were one.

INDEX OF PERSONS, PLACES, AND WORKS

INDEX OF SUBJECTS

PRINTED IN GREAT BRITAIN
AT THE UNIVERSITY PRESS, OXFORD
BY VIVIAN RIDLER
PRINTER TO THE UNIVERSITY